Brave old continent?

Why Europe should reinvent itself

Brave old continent?

Why Europe should reinvent itself

Steven Van Hecke

First edition: 2025

Published by
Acco cv, Sluisstraat 10, 3000 Leuven, België
Email: uitgeverij@acco.be – Website: www.acco.be

The Netherlands:
Acco Uitgeverij, Westvlietweg 67 F, 2495 AA Den Haag, Nederland
Email: info@uitgeverijacco.nl – Website: www.accouitgeverij.nl

Cover design: Quatre-Face
Portrait photo Steven Van Hecke: © Dieter Telemans
Translation: Ian Connerty

Typesetting: Press Point.be

D/2025/0543/116   NUR 697 en 401   ISBN 978-94-6467-806-2

Content

Conclusion

Introduction

What is the distance between Prague and Brussels, the capital of Europe? As the crow flies, it is roughly 700 kilometres – just 65 kilometres further east than Berlin. Geographically, this is closer than Mont Ventoux in southern France. Vienna is 200 kilometres further away, but for many West Europeans the Czech capital feels less familiar and more remote. For the majority of us, Prague is at best a good destination for a cheap city trip. Beyond that, we seem to have little affinity with the place, even though the city of Kafka was predominantly German-speaking for centuries and also lies at the very heart of Central Europe.

Everyone who experienced the division of Europe during the second half of the 20th century tends to think of Prague as belonging to the East. However, there is not much in the city that is non-western. The mentality is liberal, both in economic and social terms. True, there are still countless churches and monasteries, but the Czech Republic is one of the most secularised countries in Europe.

This was the city where on 6 October 2022 the heads of state and government of 44 European countries – accompanied by Charles Michel as President of the European Council and Ursula von der Leyen as President of the European Commission – came together for a crucial meeting. It was only the Ukrainian president, Volodymyr Zelenskyy, who was unable to attend the meeting in person (he followed it digitally). And what was purpose of this gathering of Europe's political elite? It was the inaugural meeting of the European Political Community.

Earlier that year, during a speech given on Europe Day (9 May), the French president, Emmanuel Macron, had already called for the organisation of a summit of this kind. During the second half of 2022 the Czech Republic held the presidency of the European Council of Ministers, so that Prague seemed the logical choice for the meeting that President Macron had in mind. Brussels was not an option, because it was deemed crucial to avoid giving the impression that non-EU countries were somehow second rank. On the contrary, it was vital that the meeting (because it was not really an organisation as such) should emphasise the bonds between all European countries. This explains why everyone was welcome, except for Russia and Belarus.

In this respect, the launching of the European Political Community was Europe's diplomatic response to the Russian invasion of Ukraine on 24 February 2022. What for many years after the Second World War had seemed like an impossibility suddenly became a reality: one country had been militarily attacked by another. The EU's reaction was fierce, but it was thought important to further emphasise the unity of European condemnation beyond the Union's boundaries. By bringing together all of Europe's most senior political leaders, it was hoped to underline just how isolated Russia truly was. Perhaps the Kremlin would think twice when faced with this united front?

The summit only lasted for a single day, but it was attended by all the grandeur that befits such an occasion. It was held in the Spanish Hall of the New Royal Palace in Prague Castle, where the many impressive chandeliers and mirrors are reminiscent of the splendour of Versailles or Vienna. By contrast, the meeting's official photograph was taken in the Vladislav Hall, part of the much older medieval palace. In fact, the castle as a whole, which is one of the largest in the world, is a complex of several historic palaces, numerous church buildings, various squares and courtyards, and extensive gardens.

This fascinating labyrinth and mixture of styles could almost be seen as a metaphor for the way the European Union works. As could the fact that the summit was held in a castle, safely cut off from the outside world.

Whoever wishes to leave the castle to visit the old city must cross the River Moldau (*Vltava* in Czech) via the Charles Bridge, with its famous Gothic towers and remarkable Baroque statues. These 30 statues look down on the countless tourists who pass over the bridge each day, making it one of the city's – if not Europe's – leading tourist hotspots.

But nowadays, that is all it has to offer. The practical reason for which it was built – to link together the two parts of the city – is no longer relevant. As a result, it has ceased to serve any useful function, other than to be looked at. Its former purpose and importance are gone; all it has left is its beauty. It has become what is effectively a magnificent open-air museum. A bit like the rest of Prague. Or – according to some – like Europe as a whole.

Europa as a museum for the world. This is not generally intended as a complement – as was clear, for example, in the novel *Grand Hotel Europa* by the Dutch writer Ilja Leonard Pfeijffer. It is still a fun place to visit. There are lots of wonderful sights to see and you get a strong sense of what things were like in the past. But none of it really matters anymore. The real power and influence are now found beyond Europe's boundaries. The key decisions are made elsewhere. And that is where the future lies. The 'hotel' belongs to bygone era. All that remains are echoes of its former glory.

Is this a true picture of Europe today? Perhaps it would be overly optimistic to expect too much of the European Political Community. But what about the European Union itself? Is the European integration project still on track? Does it still hold its appeal? What does the Union have to offer its citizens and the wider world?

In this essay I will search for answers to these questions that go beyond current political events.[1] Because there is a lot at stake for the EU. Namely: is its current model sufficiently attractive to retain the support it needs? And does it have the resilience to cope with the challenges it faces as we enter the second quarter of the 21st century?

Three years after the Russian invasion of Ukraine and with Donald Trump back in the White House, many people are beginning to realise that a new era in European history has started. The key question is whether or not our actions reflect this realisation. In other words, are we prepared to make the necessary sacrifices to preserve what is good in Europe, while at the same time being radical enough to accept and deal with our new responsibilities? Is this old continent brave enough to reinvent itself?

Essay

Unità, sicurezza,
energie rinnovabili.
L'EUROPA SEI TU.
YOU
ARE
EU
autostrade

The European way of life

There was quite a stir in September 2019 at the beginning of the new term of office of the European Commission.[2] Ursula von der Leyen had awarded the overarching 'Defending *the European Way of Life*' portfolio to one of her future vice-presidents, Margaritis Schinas. Schinas was also entrusted with the crucial migration portfolio, and this is where the problems started. That a centre-right Greek should be made responsible for dealing with the sensitive migration issue was one thing. But that migration policy should be linked with the idea of defending the European way of life was a bridge too far for many politicians on the left. For them, this combination seemed like something drawn directly from the manifesto of the radical right. 'The Parliament will not let this insult to European values pass. *No pasaran!*', threatened one of the European Parliament's left-wingers.[3]

In the end, von der Leyen was forced to back down, at least in part. The title of the portfolio was watered down to the more positive sounding '*Promoting the European Way of Life*', a move which seemed to satisfy the critics and allowed Schinas to get on with his work. For the new European Commission, this work was of crucial importance, since it represented one of the five key axes around which the Commission intended to group its initiatives during the period 2019 to 2024. The subtitle of the portfolio was '*Protecting our citizens and our values*' and it embraced a wide range of policy actions, from tighter border controls and the combatting of anti-Semitism to the roll-out of a European cancer plan.[4]

Looking back, what now seems striking about this incident is the intensity of feeling it aroused. Five years further down the line, it is interesting to speculate whether a similar incident would cause the same level of intensity today. Probably not. Because in the meantime the idea of 'the European way of life' has become mainstream. It is no longer the toxic issue it once was. This is above all because the concept has since been linked to the war in Ukraine. Those who are fighting against Russian imperialism are not only fighting for their own country; they are also fighting for 'our' values: freedom, equality, democracy, human rights, the rule of law, and so on. Or that, at least, is something that is regularly claimed. Not surprisingly, the leaders in Kyiv are anxious to confirm this.[5] Ukraine wants to become a member of the EU because the country prefers 'the European way of life' to the alternative of being a vassal state of Moscow. It was not without good reason that President Zelenskyy closed his address to the European Parliament with the words: *Care about the European way of life* (the only English sentence in a speech that was otherwise delivered completely in Ukrainian).[6] It was a perfect summary of his mediagenic visit to Brussels in early 2023.

The concept of 'the European way of life' is currently the most recent attempt to breathe new impetus into the European integration process.[7] And it is interesting to note that this effort is framed within the context of a war, which is ironic, given that the concept first saw the light of day as part of a peace project. The struggle between France and Germany for supremacy on mainland Europe sacrificed three generations of their youth on the battlefield: the Franco-Prussian War (1870-1871), the First World War (1914-1918) and the Second World War (1939-1945).[8] By then, it was clear that this disastrous power struggle could only be brought to an end within a broader framework: under the approving eye of Washington, Franco-German reconciliation was cemented within a newly integrated Western Europe. As a result, a possibility of a new war gradually became unthinkable. Peace was now so self-evident that for many years it had a demobilising and demilitarising effect. Calls to organise an effective defence for Europe fell on deaf ears. Nobody was prepared to pay for the army that this would require and nobody seemed willing to risk dying for the European ideal. This was painfully illustrated in the early 1990s, when the Balkan state of Yugoslavia disintegrated. The Western European countries showed themselves to be powerless to prevent ethnic cleansing and a bloody civil war that was taking place quite literally on their doorstep. Once again, it was left to the Americans to clean up the mess. The fact that they succeeded in bringing the conflict to an end represented a huge loss of face for the European integration project and its ideals of peace and reconciliation.[9] Nonetheless, in 2012 the EU was awarded the Nobel Prize for Peace for its contribution over six decades 'to promote peace, reconciliation, democracy and human rights in Europe [sic]'.[10]

In reality, democracy and human rights only appeared in the EU narrative from the 1970s onwards. Before then, little or no attention was paid to such matters, because the member states took these things for granted. It is no coincidence that a focus on democracy first arose in three domains that are still relevant today: the working of EU institutions, the values necessary for (candidate) member states and the principles of EU foreign policy. Of these, the democratisation of the Union's internal decision-making processes, including the first direct elections for the European Parliament in 1979, has probably been the biggest success, although there is still room for improvement.[11] Maintaining democracy at the national level of the member states has been more problematic. The so-called 'democratic backsliding' in countries like Poland, Hungary, Slovakia and Romania has shown that the Union is not – or not sufficiently – able to guarantee the quality of democracy within its own borders. This in turn undermines not only the value of the democratic requirements that the Union expects candidate members to uphold, but also the EU's reputation as a 'soft power' and 'norm entrepreneur' in its efforts to promote greater democracy beyond its boundaries. This comes on top of the classic criticism that ultimately economic interests are always given priority. In this way, the EU's development aid programme is often dismissed as a smokescreen to mask its true intentions as an economic superpower.

The alternative idea of uniting the European continent on the basis of its rich cultural heritage has also been far from successful. On the contrary, instead of having a unifying effect, art tends to emphasise diversity. This is fun for city trips, but it lacks the punch to breathe new elan into the European integration process. Traditions are tolerated but it is best not to talk about history. This is even more true of religion. The very mention of the Judeo-Christian tradition in the Preamble to the EU's Constitutional Treaty at the start of the century was too much for many to stomach. And since then, everything relating to Islam has become more of a hindrance than a help to the cause of European unity. The fact that those on the radical right nowadays repeatedly portray themselves as the last defenders of Christian Europe is equally divisive.

In addition to peace and reconciliation, the growth of prosperity through economic development and solidarity is the other dominant theme of the European integration process. The single market increased overall wealth and removed the Union's internal boundaries. Even so, the legendary Commission president Jacques Delors was well aware of the limitations of this process: 'No one falls in love with a single market.' In other words, some kind of flanking policy was necessary. Hence the need for solidarity.[12] Unfortunately, this solidarity proved difficult to arrange. Member states preferred to hold on to their own sovereignty. The euro crisis and the migration crisis had a serious negative impact on integration optimism. In both cases, the initial response of many member states was *sauve qui peut*. The resulting austerity programme and the unequal sharing of the

VIRGO
EUROPAE
PATRONA

migration burden left deep wounds, especially in Southern Europe. Of course, nothing is ever perfect, but it at least proved possible to maintain the monetary union and the Schengen zone continues to operate effectively. That being said, the price for these 'successes' was high and both remain fundamentally incomplete: the mechanisms of common socio-economic governance are still insufficiently developed and the protection of the Union's external borders is still much too weak. In short, there is no reason for excessive optimism – and that's putting it mildly. Prosperity and solidarity – just like peace and reconciliation – have clearly demonstrated that they are inadequate tools for injecting the necessary (and credible) inspiration into the European integration process.

Initially, it seemed as though the climate crisis might fulfil this role. The battle to limit global warming provided the Union with a new and powerful narrative. In the spring of 2019, Brussels surfed on the wave of popular support for this theme, particularly among the younger generation. The idea of coupling technological innovation with economic development potentially offered Europe a new story that would put it back on the world map. With its ambition to make Europe the first climate neutral continent by 2050, the Union showed that it was capable of taking far-reaching decisions. Sadly, however, even this failed to become a European 'man to the moon' project, in part because it was derailed by the race to provide a vaccine against the corona virus. In the meantime, resistance to the European Green Deal has grown significantly, so that the climate theme has now also lost much of its inspirational and unifying power.

Of course, times change and the tides of fortune change with them – sometimes dramatically. The European integration process, which once started as a peace project, is now being driven by war.[13] Where peace (so long self-evident), democratic ideals, a rich cultural heritage, socio-economic development and growing climate awareness all failed to kindle a credible and passionate European sentiment, the Russian invasion of Ukraine has succeeded. Ironically enough, the European heartbeat was finally synchronised to the clash of arms.[14]

Thanks to the war in Ukraine, 'the European way of life' has made a remarkable comeback. This conflict has released a powerfully mobilising and unifying force within the EU. At long last, the Union has a narrative over which there is seemingly a broad consensus of approval. Since then, it has only been the whingers and the whiners who dare to ask precisely what this European way of life involves and which elements of it are worth protecting, defending and/or promoting. It should not be beyond the wit of the Union to provide good and convincing answers to these questions.

The war in Ukraine

What is the significance of the large-scale Russian invasion of Ukraine that was launched on 24 February 2022? It is still too early to draw definitive conclusions on this matter? Certainly, we first need to see how the war develops. Much will depend on who wins and who loses, and that is still far from clear. What is clear, however, is that the broad principles and parameters that were set out in the days and weeks after the invasion have remained largely unchanged.[15]

Since 24 February 2022, people and politicians in the West now once again realise just how united we can be in our condemnation of military intervention. President Putin's 'special military operation' is something the like of which had not been seen in Europe since the end of the Second World War and for many it is strangely reminiscent of 19th century imperialism. Of course, this united response has also attracted criticism. Europe has been accused of hypocrisy, because in the past it too has been guilty of contravening international law whenever it suited its purposes, most notably in its support for US intervention in Iraq and Afghanistan. Likewise, Europe has not always been consistent in condemning states that use excessive violence, with the Israeli response in Gaza to the terrorist attack of Hamas on 7 October 2023 as the most recent example. It cannot be denied that the EU's approach to such matters is not always consistent, although it is equally true that the West's response to events in Iraq, Afghanistan and Israel was far from being united. On the contrary, the American invasion of Iraq was embarrassing for the Union's foreign policy. The division of opinion among the member states was clear for all to see. The same pattern (but with different member states in the dissenting role) also emerged in response to the war between Israel and Hamas.

With regard to Ukraine, the response of the West has been more unified and for the time being this solidarity remains intact. The former allies of the Cold War – the members of NATO and the EU, plus Japan, South Korea, Australia and New Zealand – have found each other again in the face of a 'new' common enemy: Russia. But in contrast to the Cold War, this time the rest of the world is not following the West's lead, not even the countries (like Brazil) that used to be part of the Western sphere of influence. True, most of the countries in Latin America, Africa and Asia have condemned the Russian invasion of Ukraine, but they have not followed this up by backing the sanctions imposed on Moscow by the US, the EU or the G7. In other words, the 'old' West is once again united, but it is also isolated: more isolated than during the Cold War and much more isolated than during the recent decades of political and economic globalisation (which was largely driven by western nations).

As a result, we are less popular in the rest of the world than we thought we would be.[16] On the other side of the coin, within Europe the appeal of the EU has increased significantly in recent times. During the pandemic, its influence very quickly became clear. For example, very few European countries chose to purchase vaccines *en masse* from Russia. The majority preferred to trust the West. The war in Ukraine has served to strengthen this tendency. Today, there are few European countries that do not seek to establish closer relations with the EU. Of course, there is the problem of the post-Brexit UK and on the continent Serbia (as so often) is an exception. President Alexandar Vučić pursues a so-called 'multivector' policy, which essentially means that Belgrade is willing to keep on the good side on anyone – the EU, China, Russia, Turkey and the Gulf states – as long as it serves Serbian national interests. In part, this reflects the fact that Serbia has still not forgotten (or forgiven) the NATO bombings of 1999 and western support for the independence of Kosovo. At the same time, Vučić has drawn inspiration from the example of the Hungarian prime minister, Viktor Orbán, with his brand of authoritarianism and political opportunism under the guise of nationalism and conservatism, whilst also reflecting and imitating the non-aligned status of Marshal Tito's Yugoslavia during the Cold War. This means that within Europe Serbia is isolated as the only country that does not comply with the sanctions policy towards Russia.[17]

Apart from the United Kingdom and Serbia (and, of course, Russia and Belarus), all the countries of Europe have a strong focus on the EU. Iceland, Norway, Liechtenstein and Switzerland are part of the internal market and the Schengen zone. All the remaining European countries are either already member states of the EU or are candidates to become members. While the Russian invasion initially seemed like the final nail in the coffin for further European integration, membership of the club is now more attractive than at any time since the fall of the Berlin Wall. Leading the way was the dramatic request of Ukraine itself, whose acceptance as a candidate member was pushed through in record time. The accession negotiations will still take several years to complete and there will be many problems along the way, but the double symbolism of this action is unmistakable: Ukraine belongs in the EU and the EU welcomes Ukraine into its fold.

These developments have also unquestionably been of benefit to Moldova. As one of the most vulnerable states in Europe, sandwiched between Romania and Ukraine and (like Ukraine) already confronted with a breakaway region based on Russian support, the pro-European political leaders Chişinău have also managed to gain EU candidate status in the slipstream of Kyiv. With the exception of Turkey (which is still an 'official' candidate to join the EU, even though accession negotiations have stalled) and Georgia (the first country in the Caucasus with prospects of becoming a candidate member), the focus since 2022 has been on the six remaining countries in the Western Balkans. After lost decades of playing hard to get on both sides, the war in Ukraine has forced a breakthrough. The problems in the region are still far from being solved, but from the EU's perspective the issue of enlargement fatigue is no longer the dominant narrative. At the same, there is a growing awareness in the candidate countries that the Western Balkans also need to make a greater effort. This rapprochement is one of the most striking effects of the war in Ukraine. While everyone thought that the Russian invasion would reduce European interest in the region, the result has been precisely the opposite: the EU has rediscovered the Western Balkans.

There are good reasons for this. And they also apply to Ukraine and Moldova. The enlargement of the EU is now viewed predominantly from a geopolitical perspective. This means that the accession of new member states to the Union brings with it a strategic advantage: the

'European way of life', as expounded by Brussels, gains an important foothold in another large part of the continent. In this way, the EU attempts to limit the influence of the other key players in the arena: Russia and China. The Western Balkans is undoubtedly a key battleground for the world's major political powers. Three of the countries in question (Albania, North Macedonia and Montenegro) already belonging to the North Atlantic alliance.[18] That being said, it is unacceptable that the EU should not be the undisputed 'boss' in its own 'inner garden'. As a result, the Union's relative weakness in this region impacts on its credibility. It is ironic, then, that all these countries – including Ukraine and Moldova – are now self-declared candidates for EU membership. In other words, Brussels did not even need to invite them.[19] Consequently, it is not correct to talk of unbridled EU expansionism. On the contrary, it took a long time before the majority of the existing EU member states were convinced of the geopolitical opportunity this represented. In particular, the Western European countries needed the shock of the war in Ukraine to pull them over the line.

In addition to this strategic component, economic motives also understandably play an important role. The market power of the EU is overwhelming. This not only means that the candidate member states are obliged to comply with the far-reaching regulations of the internal market, but also that companies in the EU gain a comparative advantage that allows them to expand their market share in new EU territories. For this, membership is not even necessary; candidacy is often enough to attract long-term investment from the Union. The local economy and, above all, local consumers reap significant benefits, as do tourists who run fewer or no security risks when they travel within the EU's ever-expanding boundaries. Even more important in terms of convincing the Western European public is the fact that their own companies also benefit, because they are much more competitive than the local players. This has already been demonstrated by the accession to the EU of several countries from Central and Eastern Europe, although the balance is offset in part by the relocation of western production units to the new member states because of their lower wage costs. Even so, this balance remains largely positive for Western Europe and certainly for relatively small and open economies like Belgium, Denmark and the Netherlands. In comparison with larger EU member states, they are much more dependent on exports. For example, one well-known Belgian bank has expanded its market as far as Bulgaria, Hungary, the Czech Republic and Slovakia, and even has a local branch within 35 kilometres of the Ukrainian border. Given these developments, what can we expect from further EU accessions? That a bank from Kyiv will open a branch on the *Grand Place* in Brussels or that a Belgian bank will further extend its network to the Ukrainian capital?

A third important argument in favour of an expansion of the EU to include countries from Eastern Europe and the Western Balkans is the human factor. Like in Western Europe, young people in these regions are relatively mobile. To ensure that they can make a contribution to the development of their own countries, it important to offer them an optimistic perspective for the future within these countries. Those who have studied or are entrepreneurially-minded will not wait endlessly for EU membership to come along. On the contrary, the lack of prospects for a bright future persuades them to head abroad, causing a massive local brain drain. This can be clearly seen, for example, in the Western Balkans. Because for many years there was no realistic possibility of EU membership, thousands of young people already left. These doctors, nurses, engineers and teachers have now built new futures for themselves in Italy, Germany, Switzerland or Austria. Those who have fewer options open to them – the more poorly educated and older generations – are left behind. Euro-sceptical politicians in Eastern Europe and the Western Balkans seek to exploit this contrast for their own political reasons,

СТІНА ПАМ'ЯТІ ПОЛЕГЛИХ ЗАХИСНИКІВ УКРАЇНИ В РОСІЙСЬКО-УКРАЇНСЬКІЙ ВІЙНІ
MEMORY WALL OF FALLEN DEFENDERS OF UKRAINE IN RUSSIAN-UKRAINIAN WAR

so that those who are in favour of European integration have yet another reason to leave. In this way, the vicious circle is complete. In the short term, this can work to the benefit of the new host countries within the EU, since it allows them to make good shortfalls in their own labour markets. But in the medium and long term it will be harmful to the EU as a whole. It is not in the Union's interests to have a series of less stable countries with weaker economics on its own doorstep.

The war in Ukraine has reminded the EU of the opportunities presented by enlargement. It demonstrates to public opinion in the existing member states just how attractive voluntary membership seems to many outsiders, who are prepared to make the sacrifices that are necessary to join this free union of sovereign states. This message is all the more potent because the current 'sacrifices' are now more far reaching than those which many of the existing EU member states were required to make, since in recent years the EU has acquired many more competences and its impact on local decision-making has increased significantly. Moreover, these greater sacrifices are asked of candidate countries that – on paper – are least able to make them. As a result, they are expected to commit to making almost impossible efforts to join the club. Of course, they continue to do so, because in the first place they know that it is in their own best interests. And who can blame them? In essence, they are opting for a near-at-hand model that offers a better, safer and more prosperous future for their own population, for which they hope to be rewarded at the ballot box. Viewed in these terms, it is a logical choice.

At the same time, the accession process is accompanied by the necessary rhetoric. Candidate member states confirm their desire to permanently join the club of the western democracies and swear to be loyal to the principles of freedom, equality, human rights, democracy and the rule of law. Unfortunately, recent experiences with certain member states cast doubt on the sincerity of these commitments. The developments in Poland and Hungary since becoming members of the EU suggest that their concept of 'permanence' is one that is limited in time. In the decade following their accession to the Union, both countries have moved systematically in the direction of authoritarianism. In the meantime, this so-called 'democratic backsliding' has been halted in Poland, but its negative consequences are nonetheless considerable, not least for the internal working of the Union and its institutions. As a result, new (and largely financial) instruments have been developed by the EU to nudge these 'renegade' member states back into line. The initial signs indicate that these measures seem to be having the desired effect: the EU has managed to bring a number of unacceptable practices in Budapest to a halt. But to some extent the damage has already been done. Regimes like those in Hungary and (until recently) Poland have caused the Western European countries to look more critically at new member states and at the idea of further EU enlargement. Bulgaria and Romania have both felt the effects of this shift. Although both countries had complied fully with the conditions for joining the Schengen zone, the governments in the Netherlands and Austria used for a long time their veto to deny them membership.[20] Crucially, the reasons for this were largely connected with domestic politics: fear of losing ground to the radical right if 'unpopular' decisions were taken.

No one is suggesting that the bar for new and candidate member states should be set lower (even though their weaker starting point means that in relative terms they are required to make greater efforts to comply). The fight against corruption, kleptocracy and oligarchical power cannot be given up – and it is worth noting that this is not what the regime in Ukraine is asking. On the contrary, the prospect of EU membership is being used to eradicate fraudulent practices root and branch. In other words, accession to the Union is seen as an opportunity to put the problems of the past behind them, providing

policy-makers with the necessary levers to push through painful reforms. The indications suggest that the government in Kyiv is serious
about this. After all, former comic Volodymyr Zelenskyy was elected president on an anti-corruption programme. Notwithstanding
the war with Russia and the lack of both people and resources, this
fight continues to be pursued. For example, digitalisation is helping
to combat small-scale corruption, as I discovered for myself in Kyiv
Central Station in the summer of 2022.[21] More important in fighting major corruption and in monitoring the state apparatus are the
many organisations created or expanded at the request of the EU.
Paradoxically, this has brought to the surface numerous scandals,
which has had a double effect. For some, they are evidence that the
battle against corruption is being fought and won, demonstrating
that no one can any longer escape the consequences of their mali-
cious actions. For others, however, they are further proof that corruption is endemic in Ukraine and will be hard – if not impossible
–to eliminate.

At this stage, the policy-makers in Ukraine seem sincere and determined. In their justification for their military action against Russia,
they refer repeatedly to freedom, justice and 'defending democracy'.[22]
This is interesting, because it means that Zelenskyy and co can also
hold accountable. On the one hand, by their own population – this is
the standard practice of political accountability in a democratic system – but on the other hand also by the international community, on
which Ukraine depends for military and financial support. This same
conditionality can be applied to Ukraine's possible EU membership.
If it is true that the Ukrainian armed forces are fighting for a country
that wants to be free (also of corruption) and wants to join the EU,
this means that resistance to the Russian invasion is not purely a nationalist struggle for the retention of Ukrainian sovereignty but also
has a wider European dimension. This provides the EU with a power-

ful lever. If Kyiv is serious about membership and continues to publicly declare its desire to stamp out corruption, this means that there is no need or reason for Brussels to lower the accession bar. Keeping that bar high can only work to the benefit of ordinary Ukrainians.

Brexit blues

Brexit forms a mirror image of the Ukrainian situation. In the latter, a candidate member state voluntarily wishes to join the EU; in the former, the United Kingdom as a sovereign member state decided to leave the Union. Of course, it was never intended that the famous Article 50 of the Treaty of Lisbon should ever be used, but it unwittingly gave the UK a perfect way to close the door on Europe in a legally correct manner.[23] No matter how far reaching EU membership has become and no matter how painful the negotiations that accompanied the exit of the British were, their departure emphasises that the European Union is not an empire with colonial allures that seeks to force its member states into a subsidiary role. Or to express it less strongly: EU membership is not irreversible. However, that is not the case with being part of the euro zone (the club of member states that have the euro as their common currency), as the advocates of the Grexit have discovered. The Greek people learnt a hard lesson as in July 2015 they massively voted *oxi* (no) in a referendum. However, Greece remained in the euro zone and ultimately accepted the EU's bail-out conditions.

Brexit has turned out to be a lose-lose situation. It has weakened both the UK and the EU. That the British have so far failed to make a success of their withdrawal is entirely their own responsibility. The far-reaching concessions made by the EU – such as the offer to remain a member of the customs union – were scornfully dismissed by the Brexit diehards. Prime Minister Boris Johnson even failed to show interest in collaboration in the fields of internal and external security. The result has been a disaster, first and foremost for the British themselves.

This mess has not escaped the notice of people on the continent. Speculating about a possible departure from the EU or suggesting a referendum to consider the matter has become a policy hot potato that even the radical right is no longer willing to grasp. After Brexit, any standpoint of this kind is more likely to lose voters than to win them. Even the Dutch politician Geert Wilders no longer insists on the need for a so-called Nexit. That being said, no one ever really thought that this was an absolute 'must have' for Wilders. And since continued EU membership is non-negotiable for his coalition partners, the subject is currently not worth discussing in the Netherlands.

In fact, the questioning of EU membership at a moment when numerous countries want nothing more than to be able to join the club has an air of masochism and even decadence about it: masochism because the resultant discussions are always painful and divisive; decadence because it suggests that we can tolerate a serious loss of prosperity (which was the final outcome for the post-Brexit UK) and/ or can deal with other forms of Brexit blues.

The departure of the British sheds a different light on the future enlargement of the EU. The counter-arguments are numerous, because they are easy to find, starting with those that serve various self-interests. Or as the French so tellingly put it: *les excuses sont faites pour s'en server* (Excuses are made to be used).

All the candidate member states together (excluding Turkey) have a total population of some 65 million inhabitants, which is roughly the same as the United Kingdom. However, their combined GNP amounts to just 10 per cent of the British. In other words, this wave of accessions will require massive financial support. However, it is not the case (contrary to what many say) that this support will need to be given all in one go, which would indeed risk bankrupting the Union. In practice, the enlargement will take place gradually: not all candidate countries will become members at the same time. Moreover, there is a huge difference between what is needed in Montenegro (population 600,000) and in, say, war-torn Ukraine. Are there any good reasons why a country like Montenegro should not be granted accession as soon as it has complied with all the stipulated conditions? This would bring everything to an unnecessary grinding halt. Would tiny Montenegro really make a financial difference to a Union that already has 27 other members? Similar arguments could also be made to block Moldovian accession. Can a country that does not have full control over its own territory safely be admitted to the Union? Why not? The Federal Republic of Germany was a member before reunification with the East, as is the divided island of Cyprus.

Of course, enlargement will inevitably put pressure on the existing rules and systems of the EU. No one is waiting for the day when the European Commission has more than 30 members. And in some domains it will become harder to reach unanimous decisions when so many member states are involved. But do we really need the accession of new countries to understand that the Union needs to work more efficiently? In practice, both these challenges must be tackled in parallel: the EU needs both reform and enlargement. Some doubters argue that reform should be implemented first, using this as means to cloud and possibly defer the enlargement issue. But whoever truly wants reform should actually support enlargement, because an influx of new member states provides an ideal lever for putting the Union's own internal house in order. Or that, at least, is the lesson of recent integration history.[24]

Similarly, enlargement should not be viewed as a monolithic process in policy terms. When they were members, the British were granted various exceptions to standard EU practices and recent accessions have also been linked to transition periods, so that the integration of new member states does not need to cover all policy domains simultaneously. Are we to believe, for example, that Ukrainian soldiers are really concerned about the Common Agricultural Policy? No, their immediate priorities lie elsewhere – and so should Europe's. Formal membership of the Union is above all symbolically important. And while there are some policy domains were no concessions can or should be made, such as reinforcing the rule of law and eliminating corruption, there are other domains where there is much more room for manoeuvre. Moreover, it is the candidate members who are on the demand side, making the negotiation position of the EU strong – just as it was during the Brexit negotiations.

In summary: given that no country at present wishes to turn its back on Brussels and in view of the fact that the EU's waiting room is currently full, this would seem to suggest that by and large the EU is a highly attractive model. In other words, in the eyes of almost every European country this model is superior both to the British option of going it alone and to whatever option Moscow has in mind.

The superior model

What is it that makes this European model and its Brussels-inspired 'European way of life' so superior? This is not an easy question to answer and it is hard to put your finger on the precise reasons. It is certainly not the case that Europe and the Europeans are superior.[25]

Nowadays, no one would seriously make such a claim. Why? Because it is impossible to prove. Similarly, it is not a question of subjective preferences, as when judging the qualities of a 'superior' bottle of wine. Nor do we wish the 'European way of life' to be reduced to the superficial level of *savoir-vivre*. At best, this relates to matters of good taste; at worst, it is all about the available budget. No, surely it must be possible to come up with a more fundamental definition.

It is likely that lawyers will point to the values expounded by the EU. These are explicitly summarised in Article 2 of the Treaty of Lisbon: 'The Union is founded on the values of respect for human dignity, freedom, democracy, equality, the rule of law and respect for human rights, including the rights of persons belonging to minorities. These values are common to the member states in a society in which pluralism, non-discrimination, tolerance, justice, solidarity and equality between women and men prevail.'[26]

Interestingly, the article makes no distinction between values (such as freedom and equality) or the principles one needs to apply to realise these values (pluralism and the rule of law). The overall impression it gives is somewhat vague and general. This makes it difficult to use these general factors as a specific explanation for what makes the European model so superior. Besides, the values in question are fundamental (and should therefore in theory be beyond discussion) and universal (and should therefore – again in theory – be accepted by all).[27] In other words, these values do not need the EU to promote them; they promote themselves.[28] If this list was the exclusive criteria for EU membership, there would be theoretically nothing to stand in the way of, say, Australia, Canada and New Zealand also becoming members, but that is clearly not the intention. Last but not least, the long list gives an incomplete answer to the question of what purpose some of these values must serve. Consider, for example, freedom. Freedom to do what? And for whom? The text of the article says nothing on these matters.[29]

Put simply, a purely value-based approach gets us nowhere. Perhaps an examination of the social and economic organisation of our European society will bring us closer to the truth? The founding fathers of the European Union were largely Christian Democrats and therefore advocates of a social market economy. Later, this became (more or less) the official social and economic doctrine of the EU. Article 3 of the Treaty of Lisbon explicitly refers to '(...) a highly competitive social market economy, aiming at full employment and social progress (...)'.[30]

This approach is in keeping with the development of welfare states in Western and Northern Europe and it differentiates the EU from the Anglo-Saxon countries, where the economies are more distinctly capitalist. Critics argue (and not wholly without reason) that the EU has helped to pave the way for neo-liberalism in Europe and (through its external trade policy) the rest of the world. This is the main focus of left-wing criticism of the EU's economic policy: that it takes too little account of the social dimension and is not sufficiently serious about dealing with the problems facing the climate and the environment. At the same time, however, the Union also comes under attack from the radical right because of the high standards imposed by its environmental policies and, more specifically, the recent Green Deal.

There is no denying that in many European countries the level of social protection is exceptionally high and that nowhere else in the world is devoting so much money to this domain. However, this latter point is a constantly recurring theme, especially when the need for healthy state finances is under discussion. 'If Europe today accounts for just over 7 per cent of the world's population, produces around 25 per cent of global GDP and has to finance 50 per cent of global social spending, then it's obvious that it will have to work very hard to maintain its prosperity and way of life', warned the German chancellor Angela Merkel at the time of the euro crisis in an interview with the British business paper *The Financial Times*.[31]

In this respect, it is important not to forget the diverse nature of the EU. Many countries in Central and Eastern Europe are not in favour of a far-reaching social policy at the wider European level. Their own welfare states are less well developed and they fear that they will become less competitive in the internal market if social levels need to be harmonised upwards. Some of the Nordic countries also oppose harmonisation, but for the opposite reason: they are afraid that the EU will harmonise downwards. Even so, to a large extent the Western European economies continue to be the reference point within the EU.[32] And the recent attention for issues like sustainability has done little to change this. On the contrary, it is the Western European countries that lead the way when it comes to integrating new tendencies and sensitivities into an existing social and economic model. Perhaps this is hardly surprising: they too face numerous challenges relating to competitiveness and affordability. Therefore action is needed to stop the 'slow agony' of decline.[33]

The way in which the economy is organised in the member states of the EU and, above all, the way in which social and ecological correction is an integral part of the economic system is what differentiates the Union from the rest of the world. It is a highly attractive model and there is a growing awareness that it deserves to be protected, not only internally but also externally. Think, for example, of the increased attention now devoted to reciprocity and conditionality when concluding trade treaties.[34]

However, the social and ecologically corrected market economy gives no real indication of the purposes for which its fairly distributed wealth and social protection should be used. Economists also prefer to leave the answer to this tricky question to the citizen (consumer), in much the same way that the rule of law says little about the purposes that the freedom of the individual should ultimately serve.

Hopefully, this means more than freedom from external compulsion or the freedom to engage in excessive consumerism or even hedonism, with all the cost that this implies in terms of both physical and mental wellbeing, and with the expectation that the expense of individual behaviour will be borne collectively. The European model is liberal, but it should not that liberal. And this is before we even mention all the different exclusion mechanisms. Not everyone has fair and equal access to a way of life based on sufficient prosperity and social protection. The final outcome of the European model therefore seems to be rather meagre. Is it exclusively for this European way of life that Ukrainian soldiers are currently risking their lives? Let us hope not.

So what, then, is the real intention of the European model based on the rule of law and a social market economy? Is it more than simply avoiding poverty and exclusion; more than providing the conditions for a negative legal freedom? Of course, it is. But the positive intentions of the European model – what purposes do its freedom and prosperity serve? – must be found at a deeper level.[35] For this, we need philosophers, pastors, writers, musicians and artists.

In the philosophical-ideological domain there are many different EU initiatives worthy of mention. For example, Article 17 of the Treaty of Lisbon sets out the legal basis for 'an open, transparent and regular dialogue between the EU institutions and churches, religious associations, and philosophical and non-confessional organisations'.[36] Naturally, many of these bodies are also very active in support of EU doctrines. The Community of the Protestant Churches in Europe also upholds the EU motto of 'united in diversity' and brings together church fellowships of the Reformed, Methodist and Lutheran denominations, as well as the different Protestant diasporas.[37] And within the Commission of the Bishops' Conferences of the European Union a network was set up to promote the active participation of young people in the European integration process.[38]

Art and culture are one of the best ways to seek new connections whilst at the same time retaining one's own identity and thereby giving ever greater substance to the European way of life. Think, for example, of the unexpected success of the book *Made in Europe*, in which the Dutch journalist Pieter Steinz collected more than a hundred essays about what makes up the cultural DNA of Europe, ranging from Abba to Swan Lake.[39] According to Frans Timmermans, this book 'has captured the essence of Europe. (...) Not the Europe of Brussels, but the Europe of the people.'[40] Equally impressive in its way is *The European Review of Books* issued by Studio Europa Maastricht, a magazine about culture and the history of European ideas.[41] In the opinion of the Italian writer and semioticist Umberto Eco a common European identity can only be created by reading the books of other European authors.[42]

To a large extent, celebrating freedom and prosperity in the artistic, spiritual or philosophical domains is something that we no longer do as a society or nation, never mind the EU or Europe as a whole. Nowadays, global diversity has progressed too far to make this feasible. At the same time, there is a growing realisation that this diversity should be cherished. Of course, the absolutisation of differences is not desirable, because this makes a reasonable discussion or an equal exchange of ideas almost impossible. However, an awareness that families, cultures, religions and other societal connections all make a contribution to individual and collective meaning should help us to find our way. In fact, I would put it even stronger than that: without devoting attention to the non-material and without the input of the collective, it seems to me that personal inspiration is impossible.[43] Tapping into these sources of inspiration does not happen of its own accord. It requires an effort. The simple presence of elements that are not solely material and not solely focused on the individual is not enough. In other words, no one is absolved from the task of leading a meaningful life.

This almost universal outcome of our search to discover what makes the European model superior seems to have brought us no further than a form of circular reasoning. It is difficult to escape generalities – and therefore meaninglessness.[44] But the road we have followed in that search has at least shown us what we are not looking for. What we are looking for is only to be found in the experience of concrete situations, which are always linked to time and place. And that is inevitably something personal.

Eine Zeitenwende

For Europe, the start of the Russian invasion of Ukraine on 24 February 2022 had much in common with the fall of the Berlin Wall on 9 November 1989. The fall of the wall – and the disintegration of the Soviet Union – brought to an end the first phase of European integration. The Russian invasion brought the second phase to an end.

The first phase was the period of the Cold War, during which Western Europe was cut off from much of Central and Eastern Europe. Following the failure of the European Defence Community in 1954 – an attempt by the six founding members of the Economic Community to create a unified defence force – and the subsequent admission of the Federal Republic of Germany into NATO in 1955, the external security of the European continent passed largely into the hands of Washington.[45] Crucial in this respect was the choice of the first post-war German chancellor. Instead of concluding a peace treaty with the Soviet Union and unifying what remained of the *German Reich* into a central and neutral state in *Mitteleuropa*, Konrad Adenauer preferred to opt for a free country with the right to choose its own allies: the United States and Western Europe (in other words, with Germany's traditional enemy: France).[46] This so-called *Westbindung* sealed the fate of Germany – and the rest of Europe.

With the explicit support of the United States, the new Germany and the other weakened nations of Western Europe – which since the end of the Second World War had lost their former world leadership –were able to focus on their economic recovery by creating an internal market, which included the setting up of a Common Agricultural Policy. Twenty years after the start of the integration process, three new countries – Denmark, Ireland and the United Kingdom – joined the European Economic Community in 1973, followed in subsequent decades by the new democracies (and much weaker economies) of Southern Europe: Greece in 1981 and Spain and Portugal in 1986.

The fall of the Berlin Wall and the end of the Cold War heralded in the second phase of European integration. Once again, the Germans played a decisive role. In the *Wunderjahr* of 1989, Chancellor Helmut Kohl's quick action took everyone by surprise and within a year East and West Germany were reunited. The unified Germany was accepted as a member of both NATO and the EEC, without the need for accession negotiations. This also indirectly implied that other parts of Europe that had been isolated behind the Iron Curtain for decades could now also take part in the trans-Atlantic alliance and the European integration project.[47] To firmly anchor the position of this powerful and resurgent Germany, a single currency was introduced and the political dimension of integration was further strengthened. It was clear that German unification and European integration were

ExpoNice

two sides of the same medal.[48] The 1993 Treaty of Maastricht not only gave the Europe Union (as it was now called) the euro but also paved the way for an unprecedented wave of expansion eastwards. By now, the EU was an important player in the post-Cold War era, a period characterised by political and economic globalisation under the leadership of the West. In 1995, the 'neutral' countries of Finland, Austria and Sweden also joined the Union, but this was nothing compared with the 'big bang' enlargement of 2004 – 15 years after the fall of the Berlin Wall. Ten new countries were admitted to the EU simultaneously: eight from Central and Eastern Europe, including three former Soviet republics (Estonia, Latvia and Lithuania), as well as Poland, the Czech Republic, Slovakia, Hungary, Slovenia and two Mediterranean islands (Cyprus and Malta). In 2007, Bulgaria and Romania joined the European club, followed in 2013 by Croatia. This meant an increase from 12 to 28 member states in just two decades – and all thanks to the Union's appeal and its ability to exercise what became known as 'soft power'. Although no one said so at the time, this was geopolitics in action. And at the same time, the Union's centre of gravity shifted further to the east.

However, in 2016 the EU was hit by a double setback: the Brexit referendum in June and the victory of Donald Trump in the American elections in November. For the first time in 65 years a member state (with worldwide prestige) voluntarily withdrew from the Union and for the first time ever there was also a president in the White House who not only failed to support the integration process but actually wanted to sabotage it. Two years earlier Russia attacked Donbas and annexed Crimea, both of which were part of Ukrainian territory. This was Moscow's response to the pro-Western protest movement that developed following the refusal of President Viktor Janoekovitsj to sign the Association Treaty between Ukraine and the EU. Back in Western Europe, however, it was still very much business as usual.

Berlin, for instance, gave the green light for the construction of Nord Stream 2, a second gas pipeline connecting Germany and Russia via the Baltic Sea (and not across Poland and the Baltic states, much to the consternation of the countries involved).

It was only when Russia launched a full-scale invasion of Ukraine in 2022 that Western Europe finally realised that the post-Cold War era of EU integration had finally come to an end. 'We told you so', said many voices from Central and Eastern Europe.[49] In his speech to the *Bundestag* just a few days later, the German chancellor Olaf Scholz spoke of *eine Zeitenwende,* a historic turning point which marked the start of a new epoch. Since then, the EU has been united in its response to Moscow's aggression, but at the same time many Europeans are asking themselves what role is otherwise left for their continent in the world. Military, Europe is still largely dependent on the United States. As far as energy is concerned, the EU has succeeded in quickly reducing its dependence on Russian oil and gas, but only by replacing one authoritarian supplier with another, plus more dependence on the US for LNG. The only real long-term solution – the transition to renewable energy – is proceeding slowly. In the economic field, the EU in general and Germany in particular are now highly dependent on China, which is emerging as a new global player, sparking off a new Cold War with the United States. The key question that Europe needs to ask is this: who will be the dominant power in the world of the 21st century and what position should Europe adopt in this new geopolitical constellation?

The answer that has been put forward with increasing frequency since 2022 is that Europe must seek to achieve strategic autonomy. In domains like defence, energy and technology the EU must become less dependent on the other major players (and therefore less susceptible to blackmail). Europe must be sovereign. Many improvements have already been made in terms of energy supply, but in the technology race the continent is lagging a long way behind. It is the United States and China that are leading the way. All that the EU can do is regulate, while its competitors create or copy. Think, for example, of social media platforms and artificial intelligence. In the defence arena, many expensive promises were initially made. In March 2022, the French president Emmanuel Macron organised an EU defence summit in Versailles to which it was not felt necessary to invite the NATO secretary-general. The meeting produced a great deal of talk but not much substance. Since then, Finland and Sweden have joined the Atlantic alliance, but in essence little else has changed.[50]

This is curious, given that there is already a strong sense among large segments of public opinion that we have entered a new third phase of the European integration process. A phase in which Europe will have to take care for itself, more than ever before. But at the moment, that is not what we are doing. There is still far too much complacency. A sense of urgency, especially in Western Europe, is lacking. We are not sufficiently willing to take up our new responsibilities in the face of this new world order – or disorder. Mentally, we are not yet ready to come to terms with the challenges that the new status quo demands of us: defending our European way of life, 'arming' our democratic system against internal and external threats, devoting greater resources to security and defence, and further expanding the EU into Eastern Europe and the Western Balkans.[51]

The situation is comparable with the one after the fall of the Berlin Wall in 1989. There were many who thought that this seismic event would change little for Western Europe. The sooner one couldget back to business as usual the better. Any opinion to the contrary was met with scepticism and disbelief.[52] Those same sentiments are now raising their head once more. Whoever warns against complacency is immediately branded as a defeatist or an alarmist. Did we not come unscathed through the energy crisis and the surge in inflation caused by the Russian invasion? Has our system not shown itself to be robust and flexible enough to overturn our former dependency on cheap Russian raw materials?

This achievement was indeed impressive and it sends out a hopeful signal for the future. It has demonstrated that when the need is urgent we are capable of doing great things. But we must be able to show this same decisiveness and vigour in calmer times too. Preparedness must become our permanent state of mind. At the moment, Europe allows itself to be led too easily by external factors, such as the election victory of Donald Trump in November 2024, so that we risk falling quickly back into our old patterns of behaviour. The lack of adequate support for the Ukrainians in their war against Russia is a classic example. This support is currently too little and too slow, because we have allowed ourselves falling back asleep by the initial successes of the Ukrainian army. As a result of such shortsightedness, we continue to lose momentum, time after time.

We need to remember that during the pandemic Europe showed that in an emergency situation it was collectively able to set the right priority: protecting the weakest members of society.[53] To achieve this noble aim, large parts of the economy and the education system were sacrificed.[54] A similar *tour de force* was achieved at the start of the Ukrainian war, implicitly sending out a strong message to the Russian president Vladimir Putin. Contrary to what he thinks, we are not the decadent West, obsessed by money and material prosperity. And our hierarchy of values has not been corrupted.[55] Freedom, democracy and the rule of law are our greatest good and we are ready to defend them. This explains our willingness to support the Ukrainian people – and to keep on supporting them. One aspect of this was the way in which Ukrainian refugees were spontaneously welcomed in many EU countries. Is this a continent that is selfish and egotistical, as the Kremlin would have the world believe?

Unfortunately, this willingness to make sacrifices and to cultivate a 'war logic' – the most obvious expression of which is military support for Ukraine – has gradually been fading away in Western Europe. We have become tired and sometimes made to feel awkward by the resistance Kyiv is offering to Moscow. The awareness of what is really at stake, for us as well as the Ukrainians, is slowly evaporating. We want to avoid the need to make difficult choices.

Is this the limit of our strength and endurance? Are we willing to risk Russia winning the war against Ukraine before we once again wake up to the reality of the situation? Are we prepared to do nothing to strengthen our own defences until the next time that Trump threatens to pull out of NATO?

If we wish to preserve the European way of life and guide it through the turbulent 21st century, starting with its second quarter, we will need to do much, much more. Above all, we will all need to show more courage, politicians and citizens alike. We must be determined to defend what previous generations have built up for us. We must face up to the challenges of the new world order and respond accordingly. If we want to survive, we must realise that playtime is over. The turning point is now.

Columns

Reading guide

'How long can Europe ignore what is going on in its own back garden?' That was the title of an op-ed I wrote in September 2017 on the occasion of the State of the European Union, the annual speech given by the President of the Commission in the European Parliament.[56] With his arguments against further EU enlargement Jean-Claude Juncker scored points with many of his political colleagues. There was little or no interest for allowing new countries into the club. The Union already had too many problems of its own to worry about. At that moment, nobody was talking seriously about geopolitics, myself included. Nevertheless, there was already a focus on what was happening beyond the EU's borders and, in particular, what was at stake in the candidate countries. With the Russian invasion of Ukraine attention for the Union's external frontier in the east has grown spectacularly. And we nowadays regard the Western Balkans as being very firmly our inner garden. In other words, the perspective has remained the same, but the manner in which we view it has sharpened.

With the arrival in 2019 of a highly geopolitical Commission under the leadership of Ursula von der Leyen this tendency has strengthened even more. Of the one hundred and fifty or so op-eds and columns that I have written in the past five years, I would like to reproduce twenty of them for this publication. Twelve appeared in *De Tijd*, five in *De Standaard* and three in the Christian weekly *Tertio*. They all have something to say about my central theme: the future of our continent at the crossroads. The selected texts have lost little or nothing of their relevance, and so they are worth reading again. Or that, at least, is what I think.

The twenty documents are presented in chronological order. Each op-ed or column is preceded by a short introduction, followed by the full reference and the entire text translated from Dutch.

Lessons in European geography

When I was a student the German chancellor Helmut Kohl made a powerful impression on me. The message of the speech he gave at my university has always stayed with me, as has my interest in Central and Eastern Europe. More than anyone the Germans are fully aware of the geography of Europe and its implications, such as the brain drain to Western Europe. This was something that Angela Merkel knew as well.

Tertio, 12 February 2020, p. 5

'Prague and Cracow are Central European cities!' His physical presence was impressive and it seemed as though his aura filled the entire auditorium. When Helmut Kohl showed himself capable of reunifying Germany after the fall of the Berlin Wall, exactly 30 years ago, his place in history was assured. Even so, in his speech in Leuven on 2 February 1996 (the university's patron saint's day) he still found it necessary to use an exclamation mark to make his point. After receiving his honorary doctorate, the German chancellor gave his Flemish listeners a very clear lesson in European geography. The Cold War might have been over on the ground but in people's minds the division between West and East Europe still remained. For Kohl it was crystal clear that the European Union needed to prepare for an expansion eastwards. The idea that the western boundary of Poland should also mark the limit of the Union's eastern boundary was for him unthinkable. The 'identity of Europe', he claimed, was at stake.

In the end, it took quite a long time before new member states like Poland were finally admitted to the Union. Even so, the enlargement represented a major political success. If they could see us today, the founding fathers of the European integration process would probably be astounded by this development above all others. At the time, it also astounded many more recent observers. Particularly striking was the accession of the three Baltic states – Estonia, Latvia and Lithuania – which until 1991 had been part of the Soviet Union. Thanks to the enlargement process, the old concept of *Mitteleuropa* was reborn, with a central role for Germany both geographically and politically. It was not without good reason that Bonn in the west and later Berlin in the east were ardent supporters of the reunification of Europe. Yet in spite of spectacular successes like the rapid economic growth in Poland and the growing popularity of cities like Budapest and Riga as tourist destinations, the mental distance between Eastern and Western Europe continues to be wide. How many of us realise that Prague is just as close to Brussels as Lyon?

Of course, Romanian gangs, a murdered Slovakian journalist and 'democratic backsliding' in Poland and Hungary have not helped to disarm the persistent clichés about the legacy of communism and deep-rooted cultural differences. To make matters worse, politicians like Viktor Orbán deliberately seek to reinforce these clichés and differences. In the eyes of the Hungarian prime minister, secular and decadent Western Europe has lost its moral and Christian compass. Brussels, he argues, does not understand the sensitivities of the east and should stop trying to give lessons to political parties that at least know how to win elections. Success stories like the Baltic states and civil protests against corrupt regimes in several EU countries fit less easily into this discourse and so they are ignored. The antics of Orbán and co serve only to widen the gulf between East and West and undermine the enthusiasm in the so-called 'old' member states for allowing new nations to join the Union in the years ahead.

However, the real victims of this enlargement fatigue are to be found on a different part of the European map. The EU's current blind spot

is the countries of the Western Balkans. The tide of recent history –
remember the wars that followed the break-up of former Yugoslavia
– has meant that these countries are relatively weak in almost every
key domain. To make matters worse, the absence of any clear time
perspective for accession has resulted in the countries in question effectively being strung along by the Union. If you are a pro-European
politician in Albania or North Macedonia, imagine just how hard it
will be (if not impossible) to persuade people of the need for painful
reforms when the ultimate prize – EU membership – is by no means
certain. The consequences are already clear: dishonest political ope-
rators gain the upper hand and the brain drain of promising young
people to Western Europe accelerates.

When the 30th anniversary of the magical year 1989 – the year of
miracles – was celebrated last year, the current German chancellor
also gave her listeners a lesson in geography. 'It is only with the in-
clusion of the countries of the Western Balkans that Europe can be
truly united', proclaimed Angela Merkel. It is not a popular message, not even here in Flanders. And for the time being, the EU lacks
the necessary strategic ingenuity to make it happen. Perhaps Merkel,
like Kohl, would have been justified in adding an exclamation mark.

And the result is once again 'more Europe'

After six months of crisis, an embarrassing display of 'coronationalism' and three solid days of heated negotiation, the heads of state and government finally reached an agreement on 21 July 2020 about a new recovery fund and the multiannual budget for the period 2021-2027. The compromise that Charles Michel was able to achieve included a number of surprising outcomes, all the more so because they came from unexpected quarters. In this article I focused on three of them.

De Standaard, 23 July 2020, pp. 26-27

What lessons can we draw from the agreement about the EU multi-annual budget and the recovery fund, now that everyone has had the chance to sleep on it?

Surprise number 1: Those who thought that the current crisis in the European Union – 'the greatest test in its history', dixit Angela Merkel – would lead to a breakthrough in the medical domain have been sorely disappointed. Notwithstanding the massive impact of COVID-19, there are no signs that a European health policy is in the pipeline. There is no funding for any developments of this kind in the multiannual budget or in the recovery fund. Nor are any new instruments being prepared that would allow members states to work more closely and more efficiently with each other in sanitary matters, which in the past has been the EU's tried and tested method for crisis management. Apparently, no one has sufficient interest. Even a budget increase proposed by Commission president Ursula von der Leyen (herself a doctor, nota bene!) was sacrificed on the altar of additional savings demanded by the 'frugal four'. As a result, the role of the EU remains necessarily confined to coordination. In other words, Europe can only take action if the member states want it. During the corona crisis there was an 'every man for himself' mentality in many member states, a trend that I have previously referred to as 'coronationalism'. Even so, the centre of gravity remains very much in the hands of these states. Will a resurgence of the corona virus and a further wave of national countermeasures initiate a change of course? We will probably know the answer sooner than we think. Whoever is planning a holiday abroad had better get ready for a new uproar.

Surprise number 2: Strangely enough, the member states have taken decisive action in a domain that is not directly connected with COVID-19. For the very first time, the member states are now prepared to break their monopoly with regard to two key competences: the making of new debts – in other words, corona bonds (although it is wise not to call them that) – and the raising of new taxes. Of course, a whole series of limitations has been built into the relevant mechanisms: no one has ever suggested that the EU would take over the financial role of the national capitals overnight. But what the euro crisis was unable to achieve and what even the sceptical Dutch prime minister now seems willing to accept in principle suddenly appears to have the status of an acquired right. The fact that the two classic taboos of the EU's recent integration history have both been eliminated by the corona pandemic is remarkable for another reason. Recent initiatives like the despised corona bonds or the financial transaction tax (FTT) have become stuck in political quicksand, but this new agreement has the potential to be a gamechanger. If the introduction of a tax on non-recyclable plastic from 1 January 2021 (just five months away) is a success, it will open the door to other new 'smart' taxes, as foreseen in last Tuesday's deal. Above all, it is the prospect that new funding will not be extracted from the EU's citizens but from the foreign companies that dump their cheap trash on the EU's single market which is likely to create support for other new fiscal measures of this kind. In this instance, corona has served as an excuse to implement old plans that have been on the back burner for too long. It is a good example of integration 'through the backdoor'. And further proof that Europe is increasingly becoming a policy-making level like any other . Local, regional and state authorities all run up their own debts and raise taxes autonomously. Now the European Union can do it as well.

Surprise number 3: This change of course would not have been possible without the pressure applied by the Franco-German tandem. In recent times, it has looked as though the Paris-Berlin axis was past its prime. The days when the French president and the German chancellor made their own agreement and the rest of the member states shouted 'hooray!' seemed to have gone forever. Until, that is, the 18 of May this year, when Angela Merkel and Emmanuel Macron laid their plans for common EU debt management and new EU taxes on the negotiating table. What a difference with Merkel's largely defensive approach to the euro crisis! And what a relief for Macron to at long last be able to put into practice one of his long-cherished EU plans! It was not without good reason that he referred to his famous Sorbonne speech – now almost three years ago – in which he set out his major ambitions for the relaunch of the EU. Since then, nothing much has happened, but after a long courtship Merkel and Macron look like they have finally found each other. But without COVID-19, it would not have been possible to pull the rest of the EU after them so quickly or so easily.

In this way, a crucial threshold has been crossed. Time and attention can now be devoted to the necessary negotiations with the European Parliament, which will give its first reaction to the deal today. As soon as this hurdle has been overcome, the focus can be switched to that other long-standing problem that urgently needs to be dealt with: Brexit. These negotiations will also be difficult, but the EU can at least draw hope from the most recent confirmation of that most persistent of EU clichés: namely, that the European integration process does not run in a straight line, that crisis are necessary to create opportunities and inspire leadership, and that the final result – like it or not – is once again 'more Europe'.

Go East, Europe!

In the early years of the mandate of Ursula von der Leyen as president of the Commission, the EU's geopolitical ambitions were very much in the background. All the available attention was devoted to the corona crisis. Enlargement fatigue was not only being felt by the EU, but also by the candidate countries.

De Tijd, 18 September 2021, p. 23

Five sentences. That is all Commission president Ursula von der Leyen had to say to the countries of the Western Balkans in her State of the Union speech, which she delivered last Wednesday morning in Strasbourg. Of course, it is important that this annual speech to the European Parliament should not sound like a *3 Suisses* catalogue, in which you can find just about everything. That was often the case with her predecessor Jean-Claude Juncker and he was criticised for it. Less is more: a good speech places emphases and must be more than a banal summary of all the initiatives that Brussels is planning for the year ahead. Because if everything is important and no real choices are made, everything then becomes equally unimportant.

Critics might point out that the Western Balkans at least made it into the speech. The British didn't. And just as Brexit was clearly not worth a mention, so the concept of 'strategic autonomy' was also conspicuous by its absence. In recent years, this concept, which was launched by the French president Emmanuel Macron, has been one of the EU's most popular buzzwords. However, it has often been used inappropriately, which has resulted in unnecessary confusion. In essence, it means that the EU must be able to hold its own in strategic

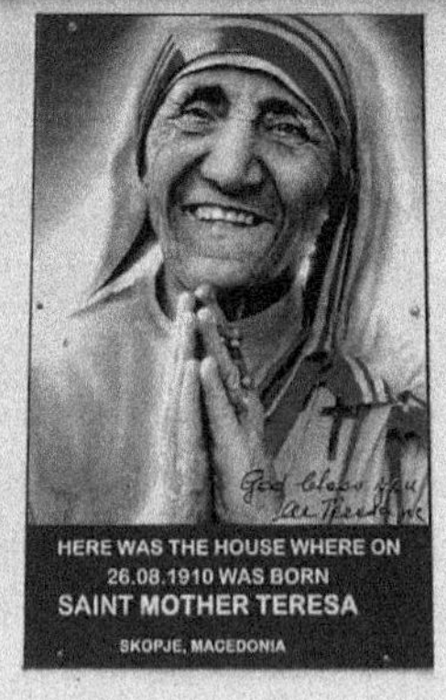
MARRIOTT
SOUVENIRS
SILCATOR
God bless you
M. Teresa
HERE WAS THE HOUSE WHERE ON
26.08.1910 WAS BORN
SAINT MOTHER TERESA
SKOPJE, MACEDONIA

domains – such as energy supply and cyber technology – without being too dependent on other actors. And certainly not if those actors have a different agenda and cannot be trusted fully in times of crisis.

Von der Leyen – the leader of a Commission that openly declares itself to be geopolitically minded –wants the EU to be able to take care of itself in all key areas by entering into partnerships with carefully selected allies. Moreover, these partnership must be negotiated on the basis of the Union's own strengths, and not from a position of weakness. In reality, these partners are wide-ranging: from the United States through North Africa to Turkey. The more cynical pundits are quick to point out that the EU is already overdependent on these countries and regions for the crucial issues of defence and migration. So how much autonomy are we actually talking about? Be that as it may, the Western Balkans is also included in that list, along with the countries of the Eastern Partnership. And if we are to believe von der Leyen, they are a top priority.

But what that means exactly is somewhat vague. True, von der Leyen announced that she would be visiting the region in the near future, but there is a very specific reason for that. On 6 October in Kranj, a small city in north-eastern Slovenia, a so-called EU-Western Balkan summit will take place and the Commission President wants to test the water in the region in advance. For Ljubljana, greater attention for the region is a spearhead in its current EU presidency. And yes, EU money will again be pumped into this impoverished region, as in the past, and corona vaccines have also been sent. According to von der Leyen, this financial support is in our own best interest: 'An investment in the future of the Western Balkans is an investment in the future of the EU.'

Visiting the place and providing support is indeed crucial. The region's pro-European politicians need and deserve some backing from Brussels, because their task is a difficult one. For the EU, the fight against corruption, nepotism and clientelism must necessarily be linked to a stringent and unpopular programme of reforms. At the same time, a strong signal needs to be sent to the young people in the region, which is creaking under the effect of the brain drain to Western Europe. Stopping this loss of talent must prevent the Western Balkans from descending ever deeper into a negative spiral.

Whether these measures will be enough is open to question. In her State of the Union Von der Leyen made no mention of a clear perspective for EU membership or a concrete timing. Even so, there is no real alternative to membership in the long run. For the EU, the Western Balkans are a blind spot on the map of Europe. At the same time, however, the Union itself is suffering from enlargement fatigue and the start of the accession negotiations with North Macedonia and Albania is still blocked as a result of disagreement among the member states. There seems to be little interest in most of Europe's capitals. But not all of them. At the start of this week, Angela Merkel was in Serbia and Albania, during what is probably one of her last official visits as German chancellor. She praised what was good about the region and criticised what was bad. Above all, she showed that the strongest EU country had not closed the door on membership.

On Wednesday von der Leyen also missed the opportunity to stick her neck out for the region. Surely that is what the State of the Union is for? The countries of the Western Balkans were certainly listening to her speech and were no doubt disappointed by what they heard. They are tired of the EU's empty words. Can you blame them if they are increasingly looking to do business with China, Russia, Turkey and the Gulf States? For a Commission with geopolitical ambitions, these overtures are a serious embarrassment in the EU's own back garden.

Merkel's difficult legacy

At the start of December 2021, a new government came into office in Germany. At long last, the Merkel era had come to an end. As she finally stepped down from the political stage, the time was ripe to assess her place in history. This was an important but by no means easy thing to do.

De Tijd, 18 December 2021, p. 23

Will much champagne have been drunk in recent days? For example, in the town halls in Antwerp and in Budapest? Or perhaps even the Kremlin? After 16 years, everyone is finally rid of Angela Merkel. Her departure from politics had already been predicted on several occasions, but this time it is really true. Even her extensive farewell tour – it seemed to go on forever – has now come to end. For the past few days, the most important EU member state has been represented in the European Council by Olaf Scholz, Merkel's successor as German chancellor. For the heads of state and government, it will no doubt feel strange to have a new German colleague and it will take a little bit of getting used to. This kind of scene is always filled with smiling faces. Everyone seems to be happy and some are also relieved. Or that is the way it looks at first glance. But things can change – and change quickly.

The numerous evaluations of the departing Angela have not spared the clichés. To underline the 'end of an era' theme, almost everyone referred back to her two most famous quotes: *'Scheitert der Euro, dann scheitert Europa'* and *'Wir schaffen das'*. As far as the former is concerned, Merkel stands on the right side of European history, because she ensured that the EU did not implode during the euro crisis. But for the latter she is said to be on the wrong side, because her approach to the migrant crisis in 2015 was ill-conceived.

The facts are not always paramount when making a summary of someone's political career. The convictions of the person writing the summary are often just as important. As are the qualities and attributes that have been credited to the subject of the summary over the years. In Merkel's case, that is quite a lot. In 2016, following Donald Trump's election victory, she was hailed as the 'new leader of the free world', a title she dismissed instantly, calling the idea 'grotesque'. Exaggerated praise and transparent insults have something in common: they both seem puerile. They also show little respect for the person in question. It suggests that Merkel can only be understood in terms of black or white and that she is somehow free from the nuances and contradictions that affect us all.

Some of her fifty shades of grey deserve to be remembered. She merits praise for the way she treated the smaller member states in the EU, following the example of her Christian Democrat predecessor Helmut Kohl. The Germans have always understood that taking into account the interests of smaller and more vulnerable countries has been one of the cornerstones on which the European integration process is built. Paris has much less concern for such matters. French presidents tend to be known for their condescending approach towards other member states. But this is something of which Merkel could never be accused. At least, not as far as her words are concerned. In her deeds the interests of German industry were usually at the forefront of her mind. Just ask Poland, the Baltic states or Ukraine what they think of Nord Stream 2, the new direct gas pipeline with Russia.

One of Merkel's weaknesses was her insistence on avoiding conflict and her continuing belief in political dialogue, even when blackmail was clearly involved. In this respect, she has bequeathed Scholz and his European colleagues a difficult legacy. The EU's relations with Poland and Hungary are at an all-time low. Her policy of trying to paper over the cracks has clearly failed in recent years. On the contrary, the problems continue to grow. Moreover, the same criticism can be levelled at her approach to international relations. Moscow and Peking both have an agenda that is impossible to reconcile with European ambitions. Even so, Merkel has always shied away from direct confrontation. The new German government has already signalled its intent to set a different course and from now on will state explicitly the issues it believes are at stake. Berlin will no longer hesitate to raise difficult subjects, like the Uyghur genocide – which will no doubt come as a nasty surprise to the Chinese. If Scholz can succeed in convincing his European colleagues of the merits of this approach, it is not unthinkable that EU foreign policy might come into line with the ideas of the progressive coalition that is now in power at the federal level in Germany. This policy would be a good deal more offensive and have a much greater focus on human rights than on economic logic. Attempting to lead world politics in all its many dimensions – instead of being subjected to it – is an ambition to which the European Commission would readily subscribe. As an added bonus, this ambition would create a task on the world stage in which the French president would be delighted to play a leading role.

Sic transit gloria mundi. It will probably take a lot less longer than we think before Merkel is forgotten in Brussels or Paris. But her opponents will miss her. In Antwerp, Warsaw, Budapest, Moscow and Peking they had better crack open a few extra bottles of bubbly to drown their sorrows at the passing of the age of Angela Merkel.

Germany again playing a decisive role in the European integration process

The events of 24 February 2022 triggered a seismic change of course in Berlin. This *Wende* can have far-reaching consequences, also for the other member states of the EU, because traditionally Germany has always played a decisive role in Europe's security policy.

De Tijd, 1 March 2022, p. 11

In the run-up to the Russian invasion of Ukraine it was *bon ton* to question the usefulness of the European Union. 'Where is Europe?' people asked. 'What is the point of European integration?' It was as if Brussels no longer existed. President Vladimir Putin listened only to what Washington, London, Paris and Berlin had to say.

As far as the 'why' of European integration is concerned, the answer is simple. After three bloody conflicts for the mastery of the European continent – the Franco-Prussian War of 1870-1871, the First World War and the Second World War – Germany was locked into an economic and political union with the other Western European nations. If it had been up to the Americans, the new post-war West Germany would only have been allowed to have soldiers within the framework of a truly European army. But because the French torpedoed the European Defence Community, their formed arch-enemy was drafted into NATO, the alliance that was set up a few years later 'to keep the Americans in, the Russians out and the Germans down'.

Even so, the *Deutschlandfrage* – what is the role of a nation that is too big for Europe and too small for the rest of the world? – continued to dominate the continent's history. With the *Westbindung*, the legendary German chancellor Konrad Adenauer anchored West Germany in an Atlantic and European alliance. The rest of Europe breathed a sigh of relief. At least it did until the end of the Cold War made possible what had long been thought impossible: the reunification of Germany as a whole. When this happened, the choices that were made again had far-reaching consequences, also for the rest of Europe. This *Wiedervereinigung* took place under the auspices of NATO and it strengthened the European integration process. This was something that the chancellor at the time, Helmut Kohl, understood well. He removed the fears of the smaller EU member states and the countries of Central and Eastern Europe by framing German unification within the context of the wider European process, so that they appeared to be two sides of the same coin. This was reinforced further with the Treaty of Maastricht and it came to determine the EU agenda in the following decades: a deepening of the integration process and the enlargement of the Union with new member states.

What happened last Sunday in the *Bundestag* might once again turn out to be a decisive moment of choice for both Germany and the rest of Europe. Chancellor Olaf Scholz consigned his country's Russia policy of the last 30 years to the rubbish bin. He talked of a *Zeitenwende*, a historic turning point. After he had already pulled the plug on Nord Stream 2 – the second direct gas pipeline with Russia – he now announced the direct sale of arms to Ukraine and a substantial increase in defence spending. Instead of the famous *Wandel durch Handel* strategy – the idea that closer trade relations would eventually make Moscow democratic – Berlin now opted for confrontation, and this for the first time since the end of the Second World War.

In this way, Scholz has broken with the long tradition of Germany's Social Democrats: from the *Ostpolitik* of Chancellor Willy Brandt to the Gazprom and Rosneft initiatives of Chancellor Gerhard Schröder. Scholz's green coalition partner – notwithstanding their roots in the peace movement – has been pressing for a change of course towards Putin for some time. And the frugal liberals have been able to sell the increased spending for defence as 'an investment in our freedom'. Even the opposition rushed to support the Christian Democrats. Not long before, the former defence minister Annegret Kramp-Karrenbauer had made mincemeat of the policy of her fellow party member Angela Merkel: 'I'm so angry at ourselves for our historical failure. After Georgia, Crimea and Donbas, we have not prepared anything that would have really deterred Putin.' This is nothing less than spitting on the legacy of someone who until recently was universally praised for her ability to deal with crisis after crisis.

Schluss damit. In Berlin we are currently witnessing a true paradigm change, the third *Wende* in a row. The post-Cold War era and the 'weak' security policy with which it is generally associated has gone forever. Germany is now aligning itself wholeheartedly with the geopolitical ambitions of Brussels, which in turn is having a knock-on effect in other EU member states. Whereas many in Western Europe are still trying to catch their breath at the speed of the change, Scholz is probably already a hero in Eastern and Central Europe. In particular, Poland and the Baltic states had just about had enough of Berlin's hesitant attitude towards Putin. But that is all over. It may take a while to get used to, but a new phase of the European integration process has started, with Germany once again playing the decisive role.

The EU and NAVO did not humiliate Russia

The contention that NATO and the EU somehow provoked Putin is to turn the world on its head. Even so, this opinion continues to surface frequently. As it did on 3 March 2022 in the op-ed 'Europe is playing with fire' by historian Idesbald Goddeeris. I almost fell off my chair when I read it and felt compelled to pick up my pen in reply.

De Standaard, 5 March 2022, pp. 62-63

'Get this, @RussianEmbassy, once and for all, in a language you can grasp. We were not orphaned by you because you were not our daddy. More of a serial rapist. Which is why you are not missed. And if you try it again, you'll get a kick in the balls.' Radosław Sikorski was very clear in his message to the Russian embassy in London. You can say a lot of things about the former Polish foreign minister and current member of the European Parliament, but you cannot say that he does not know what he is talking about. Sikorski has been known for a long time for his fierce criticism of Moscow.

His tweet at the start of January was in reply to a comment by the Russian minister of foreign affairs, Sergej Lavrov: 'NATO has become a purely geopolitical organisation which has targeted regions that were left behind as orphans after the collapse of the Warsaw Pact and the Soviet Union.' In the meantime, it has become clear how Russia is treating another of its 'orphaned' neighbours in Ukraine and Sikorski has been proven right: the 'serail rapist' has indeed been given a kick in the balls, the like of which has never been seen before.

It goes without saying that apart from Putin nobody wants war. And of course, the West needs to preserve its composure and avoid provoking the regime in Moscow unnecessarily. But Idesbald Goddeeris forgets that the current situation is fundamentally different from 30 years ago. Within NATO and the EU, Central and Eastern Europe now also help to set the tone – and this is something which many in Western Europe are still finding hard to accept.

We should not forget that the countries that once formed part of the Warsaw Pact and the Soviet Union have been traumatised by their 20th century history. On the one hand, the terrible deeds committed during their double occupation – first by the Nazis and then by the Soviets – has left deep wounds. On the other hand, they also remember how the West completely deserted them time after time, from the uprising in East Berlin in 1953 through the Hungarian revolution in 1956 to the Prague Spring in 1968. When the free trade union Solidarność drove out the communist regime in Poland in 1980, another similar invasion by Soviet troops was only avoided when a Polish general seized control over his country's army and imposed martial law. True, that was a better outcome for the West, but the pattern remained the same: whenever there were victims, the West just looked on and did nothing, notwithstanding all its fine rhetoric about freedom, self-determination and democracy.

With the fall of the Wall, the abolition of the Warsaw Pact and the implosion of the Soviet Union, the countries of Central and Eastern Europe regained their sovereignty. When asked by the West, Moscow agreed to the reunification of Germany and to its membership of NATO. Former East Germany was exempted from the usual accession negotiations for both the Atlantic alliance and the European Community. How do you think that the capitals of Central and Eastern Europe responded to these developments? Did they want to become a neutral zone between NATO and what was left of the Soviet

Union? No, they all wanted to become members of NATO and the EU as quickly as possible. Given their history, that is hardly surprising. The possibility to choose the alliance to which they wished to belong for their security was too good an opportunity to miss. Fearing they might not get a second chance, Poland, Hungary and what was then Czechoslovakia acted quickly and all submitted their candidacy for NATO in 1991.

To claim as Lavrov is now doing that NATO and the EU expanded eastwards too quickly and were therefore responsible for the humiliation that Russia is now trying to redress is to turn the world on its head. The EU actually hesitated a long time before accepting new member states and was severely criticised for it. Why this hesitancy? Because at the time the EU had its own reasons for not taking the concerns of Central and Eastern Europe seriously. The idea that a rapid expansion would upset Russia scarcely played a role.

It is strange, then, that the same reversal in reasoning is currently raising its head once again in the analyses of the war between Russia and Ukraine. In reality, it was Kyiv that explicitly asked the western countries to supply it with arms, after they had been told that NATO would not intervene directly in a military conflict that was beyond its borders. Not surprisingly, this appeal was responded to more quickly in Eastern than in Western Europe. And it was also Kyiv that made the first approach about EU membership, a request to which Brussels had no option but to reply. Imagine that the Pole Donald Tusk had still been president of the European Council. In that case, the EU's reaction would probably have been much stronger. Consequently, the fact that the EU's main institutions – which have shown great unity and decisiveness – are currently being led by West Europeans is more a cause for comfort than concern.

Turning things on their head – by accusing NATO and the EU of provoking Putin – is an insult to the regime in Kyiv and to the countries in Central and Eastern Europe. It testifies to a very narrow and exclusively Western European view of the conflicts in Europe. Moreover, this vision completely overlooks the obvious failure of the West's strategy of dialogue in recent decades. Given our comfortable distance from Russia, this is of course the easiest position to take: sparing Moscow from the criticism it deserves, while the region between West Europe and Russia once again pays the price.

What kind of society do we want?

Like the corona crisis, the war in Ukraine threatens to have a major impact on all the EU's key policy domains. Such 'wicked' problems not only trigger effective crisis management, but also raise fundamental questions about what kind of society we want. And therefore about what hierarchy of values we wish to uphold.

De Tijd, 19 March 2022, p. 23

'The time for crisis management is behind us. We can now look forward.' When Ursula von der Leyen began her mandate as president of the European Commission in the autumn of 2019, she hoped – like many others in the EU – that the period of successive crises had finally come to an end. After the financial crisis, terrorist attacks, the migration crisis and Brexit, it was high time to turn to the challenges of the future: the fight against global warming and the roll-out of further digitalisation. Because there was indeed a lot at stake: saving the earth as a liveable planet and securing a place for Europe in the high-tech world economy.

Two and a half years later, these future plans have largely been mothballed and a great deal of our attention and energy is still spent on crisis management. After coming through the worst of the corona crisis, the Russian president Vladimir Putin has upset our celebrations to mark Europe's return to the Realm of Freedom by invading Ukraine on 24 February. Since then, the EU has been in war mode, with all hands on deck.

Of course, there are huge differences between the pandemic and a war on the eastern frontier of the European Union. You cannot compare a virus with a military conflict. Even so, it is still possible to draw some interesting parallels. To begin with, the pandemic and the war are both the outcome of uncontrollable human behaviour. The rest of the world can do little or nothing to influence what happens in the animal market in Wuhan or the decisions that are taken in the Kremlin. But the rapid increase of globalisation in recent years means that bystanders also have to share in the consequences. In the past, we thought that this kind of worldwide interconnectedness only applied to natural phenomena. We have all heard of the famous chaos theory, which postulates that a butterfly flapping its wings in Brazil can cause a hurricane on the other side of the American continent. In the meantime, we now also know that relatively limited human actions can set in motion an endless chain of cause and effect.

In addition, the war in Ukraine affects everyone and everything, as did the COVID-19 virus. This is in contrast to the crises of recent decades. These new crises have repercussions for the whole of society: lockdowns limit our freedom of movement, we get vaccine jabs in our arm, we need to turn down the heating to deal with rising energy costs, our weekly shopping becomes more expensive. Everyone suffers more or less the same consequences arising from government-imposed restrictions, whether to protect us against disease or to punish the Russians for their actions. Moreover, these measures are infectious. They prompt actors of many different kinds to launch far-reaching initiatives. Think, for example, of the increasing number of multinationals that are pulling out of the Russian economy, even though there is no question of an official trade embargo.

Finally, the management of both crises has had a huge impact on all the EU's key policy domains. For example, COVID-19 had far-reaching consequences for the organisation of education and the mental well-being of young people. The pandemic also broke a number of EU taboos that had little to do with health, such as the relaxation of the strict rules relating to budgeting and state support or the introduction of European taxes and common debts. This same pattern is now repeating itself in response to the war in Ukraine. This time the taboos in question include European military collaboration, the dependence on autocratic regimes for our energy supply and the sharing of the burden for the reception of refugees, to name but a few. The fall-out of these external shocks on almost every policy domain has been astonishing.

An effective approach for dealing with such 'wicked' problems requires great flexibility from citizens, companies, organisations and public authorities. If, however, crisis management threatens to become permanent, we will be obliged to change the nature of our society. In addition to crisis management that deals quickly with the most immediate and urgent needs, attention must therefore also be given to long-term solutions. A structural approach must make our systems more resilient against both inertia and external threats, whilst also aligning them with a drastic reversal of our priorities and values. Just as public health was rediscovered as a public good during the pandemic, so the war in Ukraine encourages us to reflect on the sacrifices we are willing to make for our free society.

The European integration project, which is dismissed by critics as a purely economic story, has by and large proven itself to be robust. The EU seems to have its priorities in order. Moreover, if Europe's policy-makers can succeed in evenly spreading the burden of disruption that is the inevitable consequence of crisis management, so that the weakest shoulders do not bear the heaviest loads, this can set the tone for other levels of governance. And if this can happen, the second half of von der Leyen's mandate will have been time well spent.

Усі Ромяни
прийдіть
станьте з Укр

Todo La C

IRAN REFUSE
INVITE TO US
White House
Media
SANCTIONS
Germanent

WORLD
HELP US
CBIT

SAVE IS

The Good Samaritan

We all know this parable but whether everyone understands its message is another matter. Be that as it may, the story offers a useful framework to explain our solidarity with Ukraine.

Tertio, 30 April 2022, p. 5

Solidarity can be a thorny issue, at least at second glance, if not at first. The wave of refugees that justifiably swept over our region after the outbreak of the war in Ukraine soon raised a number of tricky questions. I immediately thought of two parables from the Gospels, which almost everyone knows. The first parable is the marriage at Cana. Many guests arrive at the wedding feast, but it turns out that instead of wine they have only brought water with them. Jesus then turns that water into wine. Or that, at least, is how I read it and I interpret it as a warning. Watch out! Many claim that they will make a contribution but there are also many free riders among them, who are counting on others to make that contribution on their behalf, hoping that their unfair behaviour goes unnoticed. Of course, that will not be the case if almost everyone does the same. In that event, the marriage feast will end in tears. Political commentators refer to this parable as the dilemma of collective action. How do you avoid people profiting from the public good without making a contribution themselves? Think, for example, of citizens who avoid paying tax but still benefit from public services: they drive their cars on public roads, they send their children to public schools, they make use of public hospitals, and so on.

The parable of the marriage at Cana does not make for happy good reading when you apply it to the principle of solidarity. Unless we really do believe in miracles, this approach will not get us very far. That is why I prefer the second parable: the Good Samaritan. Its story is well enough known. A man has been violently robbed and is lying injured at the side of the road. He is in urgent need of help. Two high-ranking Jews – a priest and a Levite – ignore his pleas and pass by. In the end, it is a Samaritan – someone lower on the social ladder – who finally comes to the man's aid. Children reading this story identify with the victim: thank goodness there is someone to help me (even though it is not the person you might expect). Adolescents reading the story focus on the hypocrisy of the passers-by: they are important people in society with a reputation for moral behaviour, but in practice they do nothing. Adults reading the story give it the most difficult interpretation: they put themselves in the position of the Samaritan and ask: 'What would I do in his place?'

In this parable, it is important to note that there is a concrete emergency. What needs to be done is urgent. There is no time to lose. Action is necessary – and fast! Failing to act because others have less (or no) interest in the problem is not an option. Excuses only serve to disguise your own reluctance and are therefore morally reprehensible. All the more so because the call for help is genuine: there is a man in need who will not survive without the help of others. To paraphrase the well-known words of the French philosopher Emmanuel Levinas: the vulnerable face of the other disrupts our 'I' focus. It is replaced by a true and direct relationship with this other in a way that invites us to take responsibility. Our personal freedom as human beings consists in the freedom to accept this invitation or not. In the case of the Good Samaritan, he opted to show compassion.

But there is something else that is also important to note: after the Samaritan had tended to the wounds of the injured man, he took him to an inn. He left the next day, leaving behind money with the innkeeper to pay for the man's further care. In other words, the Samaritan felt that he had a duty to accept his full responsibility, because he had the means to do so. The legendary British prime minister Margaret Thatcher, never one to shy away from bold statements, expressed this more graphically: 'No one would remember the Good Samaritan if he only had good intentions; he had money as well.' And having done what he felt he had to do, the Samaritan went on his way. He did not stay with the victim, but continued his own journey, albeit later than planned. In other words, his task was temporary, limited. Or to put it another way: no one is asking you to turn your life upside down indefinitely. As a result, this cannot be used as an excuse for failing to show solidarity. Nor can it be used as a reason for criticising you, because you only dealt with a short-term need and did not provide a long-term structural solution.

Conclusion: there was hardly a moment's hesitation when a few weeks ago a Ukrainian student asked explicitly for financial support. His appeal resulted in a solidarity action from student to student: www.student4student.be. This action is called 'Motivate Mihailo' and its motto is the Talmudic saying: 'Whoever saves a human life, saves the entire world.' Just like the Good Samaritan.

Who actually started this war?

It makes little sense to fundamentally question our response to Russian aggression in Ukraine. Imagine instead that for once the West is right. There are a number of arguments to support this claim.

De Standaard, 6 May 2022, pp. 26-27

It is not just around the Kremlin that 'small cracks in the wall' are starting to appear; similar cracks are equally visible in the supposedly united western front. The long-running war is starting to take its toll. While initially critical comments were confined almost exclusively to the extreme right and the extreme left, various academics and opinion makers are now starting to take the same tone. Of course, this is a good thing from the perspective of free speech and open public debate. However, the critics themselves have also come in for quite a lot of criticism. Notwithstanding a number of minor differences in nuance – one emphasises the urgent need for a ceasefire, while another makes an impassioned plea to enter into dialogue with Moscow – what really unites them is their condemnation of the approach to the crisis taken by the EU, NATO and the West. In contrast to the rest of the world, they argue, our politicians have allowed themselves to be swept along by a war-like logic and therefore they – and not Russia – are responsible for the further escalation of hostilities on the ground.

According to the online voting survey *De stemming 2022*, this self-critical discourse seems to have little public support. In fact, people seem more inclined to raise the military stakes still further.

Over half of those questioned were in favour of enforcing a no-fly zone over Ukraine and almost 30 per cent thought that western ground troops should be sent in. Of course, this does not faze the critics. They regard the widespread backing for the current western approach as further proof of the collective folly of an aggressively belligerent population. Fortunately, there are other – and smarter – intellectuals who take a different view.

Even so, it is still fair to ask: have politicians and public opinion in the West become blinded to the realities of the situation? History teaches us that this is always a possibility. Can we not see, the critics ask, that the Ukrainian president Zelenskyy is making use of a fiendishly clever media strategy to hide the fact that it is not only the struggle for democracy and human rights that motivates Ukrainian resistance, but also more overtly nationalist objectives? Even if this were true (which is doubtful), supporting Ukraine is not the same as naively agreeing to everything that Kyiv wants or says. It is also not the same as passively following whatever Washington and London dictate. To suggest this is also to suggest that since the Russian invasion all the EU's many experienced politicians, diplomats and other experts have been collectively affected by a form of temporary amnesia or insanity!

It seems more likely that Europe's approach is the outcome of collective wisdom, rather than collective insanity. Perhaps this is why the counter-arguments hold no water. Consider the facts. In recent years – and even right up to the last few days before the 24 February invasion – various western leaders have attempted to broker a diplomatic solution. In doing so, they were careful not to offend or antagonise Russia unnecessarily. It was precisely for this reason that Ukraine's request to join NATO in 2008 was politely put on hold, with all the consequences that have now become apparent. Sadly, all these diplomatic efforts came to nothing. In fact, it was probably the very persistence of these efforts that the Kremlin interpreted as a sign weakness. To argue that we should now enter into a new dialogue with President Putin, when he has clearly shown that he cannot be trusted in either word or deed, comes very close to matching Albert Einstein's definition of madness: 'Doing the same thing over and over again, yet expecting a different result.'

It is not just the empirical argument of the critics that is flawed. Their contention that the West should not have provoked Moscow through the enlargement of NATO and the EU is also unsound. Once again, the facts back this up. Until 2014 and the annexation of Crimea, the West launched countless initiatives to try and integrate Russia more fully into the European and international systems. To overlook these initiatives is to rewrite history as Putin would like to see it rewritten. And even if Putin is right, why should all the effort come from one side? What is to stop Putin himself from asking for diplomatic negotiations? Why should he not refrain from actions that might ruffle western feathers? And if he must invade a country, why does he not at least abide by the rules of international and military law? Is it not strange that the critics of the western approach never seem to focus on these matters? After all, it was not NATO or the EU that started the war; it was Russia.

The third and last main argument of the critics relates to what is in our own best interest. This is not our war, they say. We have no reason to get involved in Ukraine and would be better advised to think about our own security and putting our defences in order. However, this argument is applied very selectively. The delivery of heavy weapons to Kyiv by the West is a bad thing, but taking in the refugees forced to flee by the Russian invasion is a good thing. Of course, this ignores the fact by 'importing' the war into the EU in this manner we increase the pressure on the internal cohesion of our society. Let me be clear: I think that it is perfectly and above all morally correct not to leave mothers and their children freezing to death at the frontiers of the EU. But taking them in can in no way be described as 'in our own best interest'. Yet when it happened, the critics of the West (with the exception of the extreme right) remained silent. This is not a credible position.

Last but not least, the empathic attitude of the critics towards Putin is morally reprehensible, as I mentioned earlier. It is easy for a bystander in a conflict to hang back and not get involved. This in turn makes it easier to empathise with the points of view of those who are involved. However, the critics forget that in the first instance it is the victims of the conflict who define its limits. If those victims repeatedly and explicitly ask for help and if the number of unpunished war crimes continues to grow, it is not hard to determine what the correct moral choice should be – even if this means that the conflict and its costs escalate, both in Ukraine and for us in the rest of Europe. Or is it first necessary to reverse the roles before the critics – and all of us – finally see what is fundamentally at stake in the conflict? Let us imagine that just for once the West is right.

Give candidate countries a clear timetable

Less than six months after the Russian invasion, the EU was on the point of recognising Ukraine as a candidate member state. That took courage. But final accession will only be possible if there is no backtracking with regard to the strict conditions for entry and if a clear calendar is agreed by both sides.

De Tijd, 18 June 2022, p. 23

For many young people, the end of the exam period is in sight. Until then, pupils and students will continue to show what they are worth – not in spite of time pressure, but because of it. Whoever delays doing what needs to be done is almost certain to fail and will have to rely on the opportunity provided by re-sits. Deadlines are hated by everyone, but there is no denying that they are an effective stimulus for work. They also 'work' in the professional world.

Things would be very different if teachers, lecturers and professors set tasks with no time limit. Or if they refused to tell you the date of the exams or even the timing for finally getting your diploma. Many pupils and students would protest (rightly so) and most would simply stop working. After all, what's the point? Even those with the strongest intrinsic motivation – 'I don't study to get a diploma, but because I want to learn' – would eventually throw in the towel.

Yet this is the way that the European Union treats its future member states. Countries that want to join the club are given an awful lot of homework to do, but no one in Brussels is willing to tell them the date by which it must be completed. Result: the candidates' initial enthusiasm for pushing through the necessary reforms slowly ebbs away. Public opinion soon gets fed up with having to make continual sacrifices for something that might only become a reality in the distant future – if at all. Even the politicians who want the best for their country and genuinely wish to prepare it for EU membership become discouraged over time. As a result, they are replaced by others who are expert at offering lip service to Brussels, but are not really concerned about the future of their country in the long term. And why should they be? You don't win elections by insisting on painful change, at least not without the concrete prospect of better times ahead. In the meantime, the young and the promising are no longer prepared to wait and so they leave their homeland for a new life elsewhere in the Union. In this way, the Union effectively organises a brain drain in its future member states.

Of course, there are many reasons why the current EU member states hesitate. Their own public opinions have still not fully digested the seemingly endless succession of new entrants. And the fact that some of the more recent new members have also created internal problems (when viewed from Brussels) does not help matters. If you want to lose an election in Western Europe, all you need to do is to suggest fast-tracking the membership of the Western Balkan countries into the Union. But in reality, the price for enlargement fatigue is paid first and foremost by the candidate member states themselves.

At the beginning of March, Ukraine, Moldova and Georgia joined the countries of the Western Balkans on the list of EU candidates. In particular, there is a lot of sympathy for the official request from Kyiv, because of the war. Their candidacy is also strongly supported in Central and Eastern Europe, but it remains to be seen who in Western Europe will be prepared to stick their neck out when the EU's heads of state and government meet at the end of next week. The Ukrainians are not confident about the outcome and have launched a massive charm offensive. And not without effect, because

STOP

during their visit to Kyiv the French president Emmanuel Macron, the German chancellor Olaf Scholz and the Italian premier Mario Draghi all expressed their backing for the Ukrainian candidacy in no uncertain terms. But let's be clear on this: we are not talking about actual EU membership. At least, not yet. For a country like Ukraine it might take another ten or twenty years before things get that far. As a first step, the European Commission needs to formulate a proposal for the existing member states, asking if Ukraine and the other countries in question can be officially considered as candidates for membership. To return to our school metaphor: do they need to wait outside in the cold or can they wait in the classroom until the set of tasks prepared by the teacher eventually lands on their desk?

In the short term, the status of 'candidate member' changes very little. It is a purely symbolic political act. But this does not mean that it has no importance. It is a powerful signal that Ukraine finally has a future in the EU. And if it is true that Ukrainian soldiers are also fighting for us and for our values –democracy, human rights and the rule of law – its rulers and people must seize the opportunity to make these things possible in their own country. If they do not, there can be no question of EU membership.

If the EU has learned its lesson, it would be wise in future to combine the strong accession conditions it imposes on candidate member states with a realistic but clear timetable. If they fail to do this, the alternative is that in the long term they will help into power politicians who capitalise on the disappointments of their long-suffering people. This is the quagmire in which the Western Balkans risk becoming bogged down. This is in no one's interest, least of all the EU's. Instead, the Union must dare to jump over its own shadow and show that it has the courage to take the decisions that it knows are difficult for public opinion. It should do so in the knowledge that the EU will never be fully ready but must always be prepared to try and turn the hopes and aspirations of the candidate member states into a success.

Peace on Moscow's conditions: is it that what we want?

Asking to show more empathy towards Vladimir Putin in the current circumstances is taking things a bridge too far. Peace cannot be dictated by someone who feels 'affronted' – especially when that feeling is not justified.

De Standaard, 18 January 2023, pp. 26-27

In his op-ed 'Why don't we take a sober look at the war?' Tom Sauer says that we should take account of Russian sensitivities if we want to find a way out of the war in Ukraine. He hopes that the fighting on the ground will end in a stalemate, 'so that the minds of the warring parties will finally see sense and conclude a peace agreement'. Read: the West has got it wrong and should step back from a logic that is based on 'emotions (of injustice) and values (human rights)'.

A basic course in international politics would confirm that there is indeed no such thing as a world government, as Tom Sauer rightly points out, but he forgets that there are different schools of thought – not all paradigms place power, conflict and war in a central position – and that since the Second World War there have been non-stop attempts to organise the relationship between nation states on the basis of principles and values. Both in theory and in practice. Think, for example, of the founding of the United Nations and the role of international law. That Russia – a permanent member of the UN Security Council and therefore more responsible than other countries for peace and safety in the world – blatantly ignores those principles and values is both staggering and disappointing, but it does not mean that we should give up the struggle. The numerous infringements of this international system committed by the West and other travesties of international justice previously perpetrated by Russia, as in Syria, in no way detracts from the legitimate right of Ukraine to defend itself, its citizens and its territorial integrity. And, of course, it is free to appeal for help from whoever it wants.

Even if it is true, as Sauer writes, that 'a regional power like Russia feels ignored and humiliated by the way it has been treated by the West since the end of the Cold War', this does not make the Kremlin any less guilty of wrongdoing in the present situation. Moreover, just because President Putin constantly repeats the same old song, this does not mean that he is right. If anything, the opposite is true. The West has tried for decades to get Russia more closely involved in the international community, as Moscow's membership of the Council of Europe, WHO and the G7 (becoming the G8) clearly shows. At the same time, NATO and the EU were both enlarged, not at the instigation of the West, but at the request of the countries in Central and Eastern Europe. In fact, there was little enthusiasm in Western Europe for these developments and it was certainly not part of an anti-Russian agenda. Has Sauer ever asked himself why the countries of Central and Eastern Europe were so keen to join NATO and the EU? It was because they felt threatened by Russia. Most of these countries were rescued from the claws of the Russian bear just in time, but Ukraine, like Moldova and Georgia, had the misfortune of waiting a little too long before opting to join the western sphere of influence. As a result, they became a thorn in Putin's side. But to turn this situation on its head, as Sauer does, is strange. And it shows a remarkable degree of empathy for Moscow.

Moreover, it was to avoid antagonising Russia that Ukraine and Georgia did not become members of NATO, notwithstanding the promise made to them in 2008 and in spite of the fact that Washington thought differently. In other words, the European allies took account of Putin's red line, contrary to what Sauer now argues. And how did Putin respond to this act of détente? In that same year of 2008 he invaded Georgia, followed in 2014 by Ukraine. For Western Europe, however, it was a matter of business as usual, because afterwards we imported more cheap Russian gas than ever before. Viewed in these terms, it is easy to question whose side the West was actually backing during this period.

In the meantime, we have learnt our lesson and the West has now unequivocally chosen the side of Ukraine. At the same time, however, NATO has said right from the very beginning that it will not send ground forces into the conflict and will not enforce a no-fly zone. To the disappointment of the regime in Kyiv, the West viewed the situation with a dispassionate eye. True, more and more heavy weapons have been sent – think of the current discussion about the modern tanks that Ukraine so desperately needs – but this was always at the request of the Ukrainian government and not in response to the ever increasing number of Russian war crimes. The possible use of nuclear weapons – the ultimate argument for not provoking Moscow – and 'the risk of a worldwide nuclear war', for which Sauer warns, has been dismissed out of hand by Putin's ally China.

To now ask that we show (even more) empathy towards Putin brings us close to Albert Einstein's definition of madness: 'Doing the same thing over and over again, yet expecting a different result.' Russia's so-called feeling of insecurity is nothing but a smokescreen to conceal the real threat posed to Putin's dictatorship: what the example of a free and prosperous Ukraine might mean to the people of Russia. This is why we cannot remain indifferent to what is happening in the war and why Putin must not be allowed to win. As I have argued previously, there is just too much at stake to let this happen: namely, the protection of vulnerable countries on the European continent.

Ending the war in Ukraine on Moscow's terms without taking any account of what Kyiv wants would perhaps be easy for us in Western Europe to accept, but less so in Central and Eastern Europe and not at all in Moldova. Is that the kind of peace we want? In one sense Sauer's conclusion is correct, but probably not in the way he intended: we must certainly take account of 'more than the fate of a few provinces that most people have never heard of until recently'. We must also take account of the fact that peace can never be dictated by someone who feels 'affronted'. Sustainable peace must be the fruit of justice and a respect for human rights. For that reason, and until further notice, it is the Ukrainians who deserve our empathy – and not Vladimir Putin.

The red lines in the war with Ukraine

A year after the start of the war in Ukraine, a number of taboos had already fallen by the wayside. But crossing the so-called red lines in the conflict always followed the same pattern.

De Tijd, 18 February 2023, p. 23

Few people probably noticed but there were two destinations missing during the media-friendly tour of Europe recently made by the Ukrainian president. On his way back to Kyiv Volodymyr Zelenskyy stopped off in Warsaw, but apparently did not feel that Berlin was worth a visit, even though it would not have been much of a detour. True, the president had already met the German chancellor in both Paris and Brussels, so perhaps he thought that a third meeting was not necessary. Nor did he feel it necessary to thank Berlin for the support it had shown to the Ukrainian cause. This had nothing to do with the nature or extent of that support, but with its speed – or lack of it. In Ukraine there is huge frustration with Olaf Scholz's hesitant response every time Kyiv sends him a new shopping list.

This is a criticism that Zelenskyy can certainly not lay at NATO's door. Thanks to the Russian invasion, the trans-Atlantic alliance has been given a new lease of life. The Russian president Vladimir Putin hoped that the organisation would be weakened by his strategy; in fact, it is stronger than ever. Under the leadership of the United States, NATO is coordinating the provision of military help to Ukraine. If the members of the so-called Ukraine Contact Group do not meet on the American airbase at Ramstein in Germany, they get together instead in the NATO headquarters building in Brussels. Moreover, the war in Ukraine has made NATO seem even more appealing for potential new members – yet another of the Putin's miscalculations. Who would have thought a year ago that Finland and Sweden (the champions of pacifism in Europe) would today be NATO members?

Nevertheless, Zelenskyy decided that it was not necessary to make a courtesy call on NATO secretary-general Jens Stoltenberg, even though again it would only have meant a short detour on his way from the European district in Brussels to Zaventem airport. And again this had nothing to do with a lack of gratitude, but rather respected the alliance's official position that NATO is not in a state of war with Russia. This is a red line that his been strictly observed ever since the conflict began on 24 February 2022. Of course, the reality is much more nuanced. Where would Ukraine be without the support of the American and British intelligence services, both of which correctly predicted the invasion? Where would Ukrainian soldiers now be trained, if not on NATO territory? With whose heavy weapons was Ukraine able to launch a successful counter-offensive in the autumn of 2022?

Early on, it was clear that there was no question of NATO 'boots on the ground' in Ukraine. The request to enforce a no-fly zone in Ukrainian airspace was also turned down, much to Kyiv's chagrin. The possibility of maritime support – with the serious risk of confrontation in the Black Sea – was not even mentioned. But the Ukrainians have been given everything else: munitions, artillery, air defence systems, long distance rockets, tanks and (in the near future) combat aircraft. NATO's approach has been to repeatedly push this red line a little bit further, but always with the same guiding principle: Kyiv can have resources but not people; not on land, not in the air and not at sea. What critics of the West often forget to mention is that this support serves only to assist the Ukrainians to regain control over their own territory. If they were to do what the Russians are doing – occupying someone else's territory – that would really be a provocation. As would be the threat of allowing the conflict to go nuclear. But Moscow already knows that even for their Chinese ally this is a bridge too far.

Conclusion? On the western side some of the taboos of the past have been broken, but always within the red lines set by NATO. This pattern looks set to continue with increasing predictability. First, the Russians do something provocative; for example, mass attacks on civilian targets. Ukraine responds by demanding extra weapons from the West. Poland and the Baltic states support this demand, following which all eyes turn to the Americans and the British. The media picks up the story, putting politicians in Western Europe under even greater pressure. Initially, there is some hesitation, but as soon as the French are on board the focus of attention switches to Berlin. The liberals and greens in the ruling coalition are already convinced. It only remains for Scholz and his Social Democratic party – well known for its historically high percentage of *Russlandverstehers* (Russia empathisers) – to be pulled over the line. When time has done its work and Berlin finally gives its approval, the matter is largely decided. And so the next cycle begins.

Whether we are talking about heavy weapons, air defence systems or tanks, this pattern is always the same. As is the rhetoric of escalation and provocation coming from Moscow. After a year of war, however, the West now understands that these threats are largely empty. Just as they also now know that the Russians have no red lines when it comes to their determination to replace the regime in Kyiv and subjugate the Ukrainian people. The price that needs to be paid for this obsession by innocent civilians and soldiers is clearly not of great concern to the Kremlin. No doubt this is something that the western leaders will condemn at the annual meeting of the Security Conference in Munich this weekend. And no doubt they will reconfirm the red lines within which NATO will continue to provide support to Ukraine.

Why does the EU allow itself to be blackmailed by Tunesia?

In its external policy the EU needs to be more resolute, even in sensitive domains like migration. So-called 'dirty deals' are not the problem; the problem is that they do not go far enough.

De Tijd, 19 October 2023, p. 11

The fact that the perpetrator of the terrorist attack in Brussels was an asylum seeker who had exhausted all his legal options once again focuses the spotlight on the failure of Europe's return policies, and not just in Belgium. In one sense, we were unlucky. When Abdesalem Lassoued's was expelled by the Swedish authorities for drugs offences in 2014, he might have returned to Italy, where he first arrived via Lampedusa in 2011. Or he might have decided to try and stay illegally in another EU member state. Or he could have attacked some other innocent victims in some other country. But no, instead he came to Belgium, where he committed his terrible crime. Yet for all the criticism of the Belgian system (much of it justified), it is worth noting that the Swedes also failed to lock him up or to put him on a plane back to his Tunisian homeland. And much the same is true of the Ethiopian Okba B., who stabbed two young girls in Germany, one of whom did not survive his cowardly attack. He was frustrated because the German authorities failed to provide him with the necessary papers to marry his Ethiopian bride. A court has now sentenced him to life in prison.

The European Union's Schengen zone only recognises Europe's external borders. Not just for tourists and business people, but also for those who seek protection here and who, after a time, are granted it (or not). This means that an effective return policy must be Europe-wide. In turn, it also means that the EU member states not only need to make arrangements with third countries outside the EU but also with each other. It is ironic, then, that the Belgian secretary of state for asylum and migration, Nicole De Moor (CD&V), has been arguing for such collaboration for some time. However, her arguments have been drowned out by the slogans of the radical right, who have put forward no alternative solution of their own and are not really interested in finding one. As long as migration remains a contentious theme, these right-wing extremists can continue to blame their political opponents for operating an 'open borders' policy. They even get support from the left and the radical left, because these parties are unwilling to tackle the consequences of a mass migration that is based on a criminal model of human smuggling. A failed return policy further underlines the basic unfairness of this migration 'system': men are better off than women, the poor – who are just about able to pay the traffickers – are better off than the extremely poor, Tunisians are better off than Somalians, and Africans than Asians.

Countries like Tunisia have nothing to gain from accepting back people whose asylum applications in Europe have been turned down, at least not until we have reestablished control over our external borders and have set up a large-scale system for legal labour migration – something I have argued for previously. And certainly not as long as European countries continue to negotiate separately with Tunis about individual return policies. Why does the EU allow itself to be blackmailed by a North African land with a population of just 10 million and a GNP no bigger than that of Croatia, whilst at the same time it is more than willing to face up to no-taboo confrontation with the United Kingdom (Brexit) and Russia (the war in Ukraine)? The answer is simple: when dealing with migration countries, the EU does not have the courage to put everything on the negotiating table: not only border controls and repatriation, but also visas, tourism, trade and development aid. It is only when this happens that Tunisia will realise that it is more dependent on the EU than the other way around. Only then we will we see who is in a position to make demands and who will have to give ground.

Sadly, Europeans have a tendency to retreat into their shell whenever they are accused of racism or neo-colonialism. Tunisia is a former colony (of France). In contrast, the UK and Russia were never colonies; in fact, they were both colonisers. As a result, the Tunisian regime was treated with kid gloves throughout the negotiations for Belgium's famous return deal. However, this attitude does very little to help Tunisian dissidents or, by extension, Iranian human rights activists or Ugandan homosexuals. Together with the innocent Swedish football supporters murdered in Brussels, they are the real victims of Europe's failed migration policy. These are the people the policy is designed to protect, but it has been hollowed out by an uncontrolled inflow and a non-existent outflow. Maybe this is something that the critics – both left and right – should think about.

The EU cannot let Turkey, Russia or China take over its back garden

After our study visit to Sarajevo, Lien Jansen and myself wrote a report about our experiences. They offered inspiration for developing a clear standpoint about the future place of Bosnia in the EU.

De Tijd, 27 October 2023, p. 11

Forty Bosnian marks or about twenty euros: that is what the driver wanted to charge us for a taxi ride from the airport to the centre of Sarajevo. We did not look like average western tourists but we had the feeling that we were being treated that way. When we asked, we discovered that the official rates were clearly displayed at the taxi rank. According to our calculation, the six kilometre ride should have cost us less than ten euros. The driver made a counter-offer and suggested thirty marks, which was still one and a half times the official price. By now, a group of other taxi drivers were watching and in their eyes you could see a look of solidarity with their colleague. Even so, we stuck to our guns and refused to pay. The alternative? We moved off with our baggage to the nearest tram stop. Instead of a comfortable but expensive taxi ride, we trundled down to our hotel for just a few marks along the legendary Sniper Alley.

Welcome to Sarajevo is the title of a compelling film about the war in the Bosnian capital. And like in the film, our arrival was anything but welcoming. We talked about what had happened to us during a lecture at the University of Sarajevo. Our listeners reacted with embarrassment. Corruption and illegal work in the black economy are still major problems in Bosnia Herzegovina. As they are in many other European countries, some of them already member states of the European Union. Building a brand new airport certainly sends out a strong signal about Bosnia's own desire to join the EU, but major infrastructure works will not be enough to tip the balance in their favour. The national mentality also needs an update. And not just amongst the country's politicians, diplomats and officials. The entire population needs to be on board. Perhaps a daughter or son of the taxi driver was listening to our story. That student can also make a contribution to moving Bosnia forward, even if it is only to avoid the next western visitor having his or her prejudices confirmed. Helping to achieve EU membership is everyone's business.

It is also a very long process. Just years after the signing of the 1995 Daytona agreement that brought the Bosnian civil war to an end, the EU emerged as an important partner in the country's reconstruction. In 2004, the Union took over the leadership of the peacekeeping force that supervised compliance with the Daytona agreement. However, internal division meant that it was not until 2016 that Bosnia and Herzegovina officially applied to become a member of the EU. Completing and returning the European Commission's questionnaire to Brussels took another three years. In comparison, it recently took Ukraine just a few weeks to complete theirs. In other words, Bosnia has wasted more than a decade. Ironically enough, it was the war in Ukraine that has finally speeded things up. Since the Russian invasion, enlargement is once again high on the agenda of the EU and this has worked to the advantage of the countries in the Western Balkans. To the surprise of many, at the end of last year Bosnia was officially granted the status of candidate, along with Ukraine and Moldova.

236-L
CEE
CANNED
BEEF
SPOMENIK
MEĐUNARODNOJ
ZAJEDNICI
ZAHVALNI GRAĐANI SARAJEVA

The accession of new member states is not universally popular in the EU, above all in Western Europe. The effects of the last phase of enlargement have not yet been fully digested, while democratic backsliding in Poland and Hungary and the generally negative image of the Western Balkans do not help. Part of the problem is that the political rulers in these countries only pay lip service to the EU. No politician wants to ask his people to make great sacrifices when the ultimate reward – EU membership – often seems impossibly distant. In other words, the EU is also part of the problem. The Union rightly insists that the conditions for accession cannot be diluted, but even when they have been fulfilled candidate countries are still left in the dark about when they might actually join the club. In short, there is a need for greater clarity and political leadership on both sides. This is the only way to achieve a win-win outcome.

As an EU member state, Bosnia would finally be able to offer permanent peace and stability to its citizens. For the EU, Bosnian accession would be a step towards realising the Union's geopolitical ambitions. For Brussels, there is a lot at stake. The Western Balkans are part of the Union's own back garden, so it would be a strategic disaster if they fell under the influence of Turkey, Russia, the Gulf states or China instead. Likewise, the excessive and detrimental interference of Serbia must also be held in check. At the same time, the region offers numerous opportunities for our economy. It is far more likely that a Flemish company will become active in Bosnia than a Bosnian bank will become active in Flanders. Last but not least, we also have a moral obligation to give the younger generations in the Western Balkans a hopeful outlook for the future.

At the start of next month, the European Commission will announce which candidate countries are deemed to have made sufficient progress to move on to the next stage of the EU accession procedure. In December, a meeting of the EU's heads of state and government will make a decision based on these recommendations. It will take courage to stand up to the criticisms of the many opponents of EU enlargement, just as it will take courage not to water down the accession requirements, whilst at the same time offering the countries in question a concrete perspective. A bit like the student who approached us after the lecture and offered without blushing to give us a ride back to the airport in his own car.

Urgently needed: European leadership

In the run-up to the Belgian presidency of the Council of the European Union in the first half of 2024, I pleaded for Flemish and federal ministers to show more courage. Why? Because in general they seemed reluctant to say anything meaningful about current EU issues or the future of the Union as a whole.

De Tijd, 27 December 2023, p. 11

'The European presidency in 2024 will mark the culmination of a whole series of in-depth economic, social and environmental reforms that are intended to modernise our country.' This bold statement did not come from the last week's annual Christmas address given by King Philip, because the monarch did not say a single word about Europe or about the approaching Belgian presidency of the European Council. Besides, such a prediction coming from the king's mouth would hardly have sounded credible. No, the comment was made by Alexander De Croo (Open VLD) and Paul Magnette (PS) at the end of September 2020, when the new federal government at long last came into office. In their coalition agreement they set ambitious targets at the European and international levels. They even devoted a whole section of the document to: 'Belgium, a strong voice in Europe and the world'. Flanked by the EU flag and two Belgian tricolours on the imposing staircase of the Egmont Palace, Magnette praised De Croo's *vraie capacité de leadership*.

A year earlier, the Flemish Government had set the tone in its own coalition agreement, in which the references to Europe and the 2024 presidency were more numerous and more concrete. Once again, the bar was set high: 'To set an ambitious and impactful Flemish-European policy that contributes to an effective and widely endorsed European Union that supports its citizens and companies.'

What has been achieved since then? As 2024 approaches, have the two governments – one federal, one regional – done what is necessary to get the presidency off to a flying start? There is certainly no denying that in recent months the national and Flemish diplomats have worked themselves into a feverish sweat. Not only to get everything ready before 1 January, but also (and above all) to limit the damage that their own ministers have caused. The many times in recent years that Belgium has been unable to take a unified position on EU matters because of internal differences can no longer be counted on the fingers of both hands. This was usually because of a clash between the Flemish and federal governments, often over climate measures. These clashes yielded political popularity at the domestic level, but at the EU level it was the diplomats and officials who were left to pick up the pieces. The reputational damage among the other EU member states was considerable. Why should the Union take any account of Flanders and Belgium if we can never make up our minds on key European issues?

Equally harmful is the resulting impression that Europe imposes decisions on us that we can do little or nothing to change. It is almost as if we are not consulted. But we are. We are involved in every stage of the decision-making process, from the preparatory work groups to the final meeting of the relevant European ministers. For all that, it sometimes seems as though Flanders and Belgium are not an integral part of the European Union. And then we complain that the EU is unknown and unloved in our region and country! This is the same as the mayor of a medium-sized Flemish city who complains about an excess of Flemish regulations, even though he has sat in the Flemish Parliament for many years but done nothing about it – and then he wonders why the Flemish level does not get the respect it deserves among his voters. Hmm.

Not surprisingly, the policy results of this non-approach are disappointing. We are the EU champion of belatedly or incorrectly implementing EU regulations and in 2024 there is a good chance that we will be censured by the EU because of the unacceptable size of our budget deficit. In other words, Belgium can hardly be called a model member state. What we are good at is defending the interests of our companies, as witnessed by the success of keeping the Antwerp diamond sector out of the sanctions package against Russia for as long as possible. And rightly so, because our prosperity is dependent to a large extent on our trade within the European single market. In short, there is a lot at stake. Fortunately, our politicians have understood this.

But you don't need an EU Council presidency to make this happen. Our interests should be on the radar at all times and in all places. No, giving leadership to the EU means something else. Not more navel gazing with ever greater conviction, but making clear how Flanders and Belgium wants to give shape to the EU in the years ahead. What priorities do we wish to set? Where should the EU try to take the lead in our increasingly unstable world? What is our vision for the future of the continent? More concretely, how can we make a success of the forthcoming enlargement of the Union – for example, with Ukraine? The coming six months are an ideal opportunity to ditch the stale (and frequently embarrassing) platitudes about 'feasibility' and 'affordability'. The time is over for meaningless slogans or simply repeating what other heads of state and government have already said. In the first half of next year, our politicians must show that they are capable of much better than that. It is only once in a political generation that we get the chance to take the reins of European leadership. Let's not waste it.

At the start of this month in his final interview, the late and sadly missed Dutch professor Mathieu Segers made a similar appeal for greater European leadership: 'Europe needs to make a massive change of course, but it is not happening quickly enough.' For that reason, honoured Flemish and federal excellencies, get your finger out! Leave your comfort zone. Rediscover the ambitions you had in your coalition agreements. Surprise us. And the rest of the EU.

With the migration pact the EU has set a significant new course

For the radical right it fails to go far enough; for others the European migration pact is wholly immoral. But because the EU is dependent on third countries, so-called 'dirty deals' are unavoidable. The only alternative to this *Realpolitik* is the status quo: smuggling, exploitation and human trafficking.

De Standaard, 4 January 2024, p. 28

We all like to sing our own praises from time to time, especially if a long hoped-for breakthrough finally becomes a reality. At the end of 2023, it rained superlatives when the European Parliament and the member states reached agreement on the European migration pact shortly before the Christmas recess.

This success was more than welcome, because it seemed likely that the year would end in disappointment for the EU. At the European summit in Brussels just a few days earlier the only point of consensus related to the accession negotiations with Ukraine. This, however, was a pyrrhic victory, since it does nothing to provide President Volodymyr Zelenskyy with the weapons and ammunition he needs. As far as extra money for Ukraine was concerned – to pay his soldiers, teachers and officials – the Hungarian prime minister Viktor Orban refused to budge an inch. So making progress on migration – a domain where Orban traditional likes to play the firebrand – was a pleasing bonus. Commission president Ursula von der Leyen spoke of an 'historic agreement'.

On the other side of the *Rue de la Loi*, the Belgian Secretary of State for Asylum and Migration Nicole de Moor pre-empted the agreement and its likely effects by claiming that it would reduce the number of asylum seekers in Belgium by two-thirds. Really? 'This calculation seems rather simplistic', commented *De Standaard* (16 December) succinctly. Indeed, a quick calculation of this kind does nothing to guarantee that the European migration pact will have an immediate effect on the ground or that all the member states will be willing to cooperate with its provisions.

These doubts are not groundless. In the past, some of the member states refused to abide by the conditions that had been agreed. Moreover, no one is in a position to guarantee that the total number of illegal border crossings will decrease in the future. If Belgium only needs to provide for a relatively small proportion of reception facilities but if migration pressure remains high, the absolute figures for incoming migrants might actually increase. In that case, there is little doubt which party De Moor will attack in her defence.

The competent European Commissioner, Margaritis Schinas, has pointed out (probably unintentionally) that the breakthrough only relates to five of the fourteen sections of the migration pact. Seven sections had already been dealt with previously. The remaining two sections will not be finalised before the end of the Commission's 2019-2024 legislature. In particular, the failure to reach agreement on the guidelines for repatriation – how can the member states better align their return policies? – is worrying. This Achilles' heel of the migration pact should have served as the culmination of a truly common approach: an integrated European policy for the arrival and return of migrants. On the other hand, this lacuna should not detract from the fact that agreement about the pre-entry screening of all people who arrive at the EU's borders and the obligation for solidarity between the member states are significant achievements.

For those of you who have forgotten, the migration problem has been dragging on for almost a decade and the European Commission proposed its package of new measures as long ago as September 2020. But as this legislature now approaches its end, it is fair to say that the Commission has managed to set a new course in this extremely difficult and sensitive domain.

As a result, much of the gloom and doom that has greeted the new agreement is misplaced. Many of the commentators claim that the negotiators have achieved nothing of substance. 'The only merit of the agreement is that it exists', wrote *De Standaard* in its editorial of 22 December. The online version of the editorial was introduced with the telling comment: 'The migration theme will only lose its electoral power when Europe gains control over the migration flow.' Read: the glass is half full, because 'Europe cannot maintain its level of prosperity without labour migration.' That is the truth, no matter how unpalatable for some. It is no longer sufficient to implement a common border policy and to use the asylum system exclusively for those for whom it is intended. There is an urgent need for a European system of mass and legal labour migration. In November, the European Commission put forward far-reaching proposals on this matter, but the chances of reaching swift agreement are almost non-existent.

For Arnon Grunberg (writing in *De Standaard* on 23 December) the glass is completely empty. According to the Dutch commentator, the European migration pact is nothing more than 'pretentious absurdism which criminalises asylum seekers under a veneer of window dressing that seeks to hide the total lack of European solidarity'. Of course, it has to be admitted that some points of the new agreement are morally questionable. But what is the alternative? Does it not make sense to focus on the points that can gain the backing of a sufficient number of countries and a majority in the European Parliament? And have the member states (nota bene currently under the leadership of a centre-left government in Spain) and the MEPs from the centre parties that made an agreement possible really strayed from the straight and narrow?

The truth of the matter is simple: at the present time, the only alternative to the migration pact is the status quo. And in the absence of effective policy, that is a model led by criminals who will stop at nothing. They run a 'system' of smuggling, exploitation and human trafficking, which (to make matters even worse) is fundamentally unfair. Because in this system men are better off than women and the poor are better off than the extremely poor. As are Tunisians over Somalis and Africans over Asians. It is a non-policy that makes no distinction between labour migration and the protection of asylum seekers. And God help you if you are an Iranian human rights activist or a Ugandan homosexual... It is these things – and not the migration pact – that the so-called left wing intellectuals should really be getting worked up about.

Creating false expectations or misidentifying the real enemy will get us nowhere. Instead, the emphasis must be on solidarity within Europe and priority for the weakest. To make this possible, we need to enforce – you can call it 'take back control' if you like – an integrated policy that is both transparent and honest. Such a policy will not convince everyone, nor will it solve all the problems. But every step that takes us in this direction deserves respect and encouragement.

A tough old bird

Still bursting with health, NATO – founded in 1949 – celebrated its 75th birthday in 2024. Even in the absence of a European defence capability, the trans-Atlantic alliance is still alive and kicking. And all thanks to the Russian president Vladimir Putin. And notwithstanding decades of European integration.

Tertio, 3 April 2024, p. 5

'Brain dead'. That is how Emmanuel Macron described NATO at the end of 2019. His interview in *The Economist* caused quite a stir, not least in Brussels, where the alliance has its headquarters. That the French president chose to vent his sharp criticism in the Anglo-Saxon press was hardly a coincidence. With Donald Trump in the White House, Europe was confronted for the first time with an American president who refused to unconditionally back trans-Atlantic solidarity. This is a serious problem, since Article 5 of the NATO treaty – an attack on one member state is an attack on all the others – is the cornerstone of the organisation. And following the British withdrawal from the European Union, London has also been lost as a reliable partner.

Macron's opinion received strong support in many circles, not least because his words effectively reopened a number of old wounds. Should the West's defensive alliance against the Soviet Union not have been disbanded at the end of the Cold War, as was the case with the Warsaw Pact? Why was it necessary for the alliance's members to search for 'artificial' new objectives – like the combatting of international terrorism – in order to remain relevant? Surely the fact that between 2003 and 2021 NATO was charged by the United Nations with leading a large-scale operation in Afghanistan proved that the organisation had no function within its own territorial jurisdiction?

What few people now remember about Macron's interview is that he also called on the European Union to take urgent action to put its own defence in order. The British and the Americans could no longer be relied on 100% and it was time to wake up to this new reality before it was too late. If Europe wanted to effectively defend its interests in the wider world, it could only do so as an autonomous and self-supporting geopolitical power, according to the French president. Perhaps more surprisingly, the German chancellor Angela Merkel also shared this assessment, although she expressed it in less forceful terms. Following yet another failed summit with the unpredictable Trump in 2017, she commented during the annual beer festival in Munich that 'Europe needs to take its fate into its own hands.'

When the pro-European Joe Biden became US president, this sense of urgency evaporated. However, there was no return to the good old days of the past. When Biden decided to pull all American troops out of Afghanistan, which unilaterally terminated the NATO mission, he did not even feel it was necessary to consult with the British beforehand. Equally embarrassing was the fact that the other European countries were unable to get their own citizens out of Kabul without the help of Washington.

All this changed on 24 February 2022. The Russian invasion of Ukraine catapulted NATO back into a leading role. Who else would be able to offer Kyiv the military support it needed? For the EU, it was again painful that it were the Americans and the British who took the lead in this new European conflict, almost as though nothing had changed in the 80 years since the end of the Second World War. Even so, Macron invited his fellow European leaders to a defence summit in Versailles, to which he pointedly neglected to invite the United States, the United Kingdom and the secretary-general of NATO. The summit produced much talk but little action, since then the situation has remained largely the same, with the exception of the accession of Finland (a neighbour of Russia) and Sweden (the champion of European pacifism) to the alliance.

So Macron was wrong. And all thanks to Vladimir Putin. His invasion had the opposite effect to what he expected. NATO has been resurrected and is bursting with confidence. Old the alliance may be, but it is by no mean past it. As it celebrates the 75th anniversary of its founding, there are fewer doubts about the reasons for its existence than ever before, especially in Central and Eastern Europe. Yet at the same time Macron also hit the nail on the hear: Europe urgently needs to learn how to take care of itself. The time for talking has long gone. No one is suggesting the Europe should build up a serious offensive capability. But developing a capability to defend ourselves against Moscow's attacks – on the ground in Ukraine and in hybrid form elsewhere in Europe – is absolutely essential. This in no way excludes the possibility of close NATO collaboration. The new watchword must be: together if we can, separately if we can't.

BIBLIOTEKA

Radicalisation and normalisation are not compatible

In the run-up to the European elections of 2024, many eyes were focused on the continuing rise of the radical right. Equally important is the way in which other parties respond to this development. Are they driving all different kinds of factions into each other's arms or are they seeking to exploit the internal contradictions as much as they can?

De Tijd, 30 May 2024, p. 11

Political parties are not pawns on a chess board. They cannot change position abruptly. Credibility is one of their key necessities and you can never know how your own voters are going to react. Moreover, the idea of a game of chess presupposes stability, fixed rules and predictability. None of these things exist in politics.

During an election campaign, we are constantly reminded about that. How can parties remain true to themselves and yet still project a newness that they hope will attract additional voters? Even the most minor change of course in a strategy or programme is meticulously studied and subjected to extensive commentary.

Of course, parties can and do change, but as a rule it has to happen gradually. Their actions are not separate from society and they react above all in relation to each other. Or else they closely monitor parties abroad and attempt to copy their successes at home.

At the European level, all these different elements come together. The various national positions are added up to create European political families. And in the EU, everyone flirts with everyone. Old friendships, short-term affairs, long-term marriages, adultery, blackmail and infidelity: they are all an integral part of the European political game.

In this way, for example, the party of the Hungarian prime minister Viktor Orbán slammed the door in the face of the European People's Party (EPP) after 17 years of collaboration. A painful divorce was inevitable after *Fidesz* – which first saw the light of day as a left-liberal formation – continued to move further and further to the right. Since then, party has not really belonged anywhere – its current EU status is non-attached – and this notwithstanding Orbán's constant threats to set up an alternative right-wing formation.

In recent times, this dream of a rightist alliance has resurfaced but it seems unlikely to happen. While *Fidesz* and parties like the *Lega* of Matteo Salvini and *Alternative für Deutschland* (AfD) continue to radicalise further, the *Rassemblement National* of Marine Le Pen is moving back closer to the centre. In the hope of winning the 2027 French presidential election, Le Pen believes that every sacrifice is necessary, even if it means becoming more mainstream and socially acceptable.

This explains the recent break with the AfD, which represents a significant blow to the idea of creating a single European family on the political right. These two tendencies – radicalisation and normalisation – are not compatible. Essentially, this comes down to the question of on which side of the 'European' firewall you want to stand: do you want to be on the side of the radical right or do you want to be on the side of the respectable right, whose leading representative at the moment is the Italian prime minister Georgia Meloni. This distinction is fundamental: one side has respect for the rule of law and democracy, is committed to trans-Atlantic solidarity as embodied in NATO and supports Ukraine in its war against Russia; the other side does not.

This firewall also explains which side the EPP is willing to work with in order to help Ursula von der Leyen secure a second mandate as Commission President. And the more the left takes offence at this, the more they drive all shades of the right into each other's arms.

The current turbulence looks set to last for a while. During the campaign season, parties often fail to offer much of real substance to hold on to. *Panta rhei*; everything flows. This is something that Heraclitus already knew over 2,500 years ago. It will be Europe's voters who determine the river bed in which the different parties will be allowed to flow during the next five years.

Russia now threatens to triumph in Moldova as well

The battle between Russia and West to expand their respective spheres of influence is also being fought at the ballot box. This is currently the case in Moldova, a country that wishes to emerge from the grey zone in which it finds itself. There is a lot at stake and Russia will do all it can to tip the balance in its favour – or so I wrote in the run-up to the presidential elections in 2024.

De Tijd, 16 August 2024, p. 9

Agents of the state security service carrying out a raid on the national parliament of a candidate country of the European Union in broad daylight? This is what happened in Moldova – the poorest country on the European continent – at the start of August 2024. During the raid, Ion Creanga was arrested and handed over to the public prosecutor of the anti-corruption ministry. Creanga is not just anybody: he is a senior official who has been the head of the parliament's legal department for more than 30 years. So why was he arrested? Because it seems that throughout that period he has been working on behalf of the regime of Vladimir Putin. He systematically provided the Russian embassy with crucial inside information about the ins and outs of Moldovian politics. On the day that Creanga's luck finally ran out, a Moldovian policeman was also put on a plane to Moscow. It appears that he too had been leaking sensitive material to Moscow about the border crossing with Transnistria. Transnistria is a breakaway region within Moldova, where a pro-Russian regime artificially maintains a microstate.

As in neighbouring Ukraine, this fight on two fronts – against corruption and against Russian interference – is doomed. It is a case of you're damned if you do and you're damned if you don't. If the Moldovian government takes no action, the critics are lining up to lambast reluctant or incompetent state agencies. If successful action is taken, this is seen as further evidence of the endemic and deep-seated nature of corruption in Moldovian society. Even so, the government has no alternative. If countries like Moldova and Ukraine are serious about EU membership, they will only be accepted if fraudulent practices are eradicated root and branch. And it is a battle that they will need to wage continually – and not simply because Brussels will not give them an inch of leeway. True, the 'fundamentals first' approach of the European Commission, which means that the democratic rule of law needs to be in place before accession negotiations about domains like the economy and education can begin, is indeed designed specifically to underline the crucial importance of the need to combat corruption and foreign interference. But the Moldovian and Ukrainian leaders also know that it is in their country's own interests. It is the only guarantee that the younger generations will be able to build up a decent, honest and worthwhile life on their home soil.

In one sense, it is remarkable that the powers-that-be in Kyiv have succeeded (more or less) in mobilising their scarce human and financial resources to tackle the country's legendary corruption, while at the same time fighting a national war of survival. Moldova does not have the major disadvantage of a war to cope with, but it faces other problems that are equally intractable. As a small country with a population of just 2.5 million, wedged between two large neighbours in the form of Russia and Ukraine, Moldova simply does not have the capacity to defend itself against the hybrid war that Russia is waging. Moscow doesn't even need to fire a single shot. The dissemination of disinformation and fake news is much more cost effective. The

Kremlin's intention is clear: to destabilise the country from the inside out and in this way to systematically sabotage the steady process of rapprochement with the EU.

In the short term, there is a lot at stake for Moldova. The first round of the presidential elections takes place on 20 October. There are already a number of pro-Russian candidates to challenge the current president, Maia Sandu. This pro-European and pro-Western politician will probably have to go to a second round, because her popularity is fading. To underline precisely what is at issue, Sandu has organised a referendum on EU membership to coincide with the presidential election. Moldova has been a candidate country since 2022. At the end of 2023, the EU heads of state and government decided that the country is ready to start accession negotiations. At the end of June 2024, during the Belgian Council presidency, these negotiations were officially started. Many people played a part in making this diplomatic success possible and Sandu was certainly one of them. She now hopes to exploit this success politically, knowing that the majority of the Moldovians are in favour of EU membership.

Observers expect a pyrrhic victory for Sandu, because new parliamentary elections are due to be held in the spring of 2025 and it is unlikely that she will be able to secure a majority that will support her drastic reform agenda. This will effectively take Moldova back to square one. Of course, lip service will continue to be paid to the EU and its ideals, but in practice Russia will have won. This is similar to the situation in Georgia, where the holders of power are all pro-Russian, while the younger generations demonstrate in the capital Tiblisi by waving their EU flags.

There are also plenty of EU flags in Moldova. You can see them everywhere in the capital city Chişinău. You might be mistaken for thinking that the country has already joined the Union. That is what the leaders of 44 countries must also have thought in mid-2023 when they gathered in Moldova to hold the second meeting of the European Political Community. President Sandu received her colleagues in Mimi, a magnificent wine chateau some 50 kilometres from the capital and not far from the border with Transnistria. In general, the condition of Moldovian roads is terrible, but the road from the airport to the chateau was as smooth as glass. Even so, a layer of new asphalt cannot hide the fact that Moldova needs a deeper and more painful transformation – unless Moscow plans to take over control.

ТРЕТЬЕМУ СЪЕЗДУ СОВЕТОВ
В АВГУСТЕ 1921 г
НА III СЪЕЗДЕ СОВЕТ
Тираспольского уе
М. В. Ф
изб
ПОЧЕТНЫМ

Time for a new Team Europe

Instead of losing time in unnecessary masochism, Europe needs to find political leaders who will dare to stand up to Donald Trump and offer resistance to what the EU expects to happen following his victory in the US presidential elections.

De Tijd, 15 November 2024, p. 11

The Germans need to wait a hundred days before they can elect a new federal parliament. On 23 February 2025, our neighbours to the east will go to the ballot box. If the opinion polls are correct, it seems probable that the current chancellor Olaf Scholz will lose his job. His most likely successor is the Christian Democrat Friedrich Merz. Germany urgently needs a new leader, because the country is facing huge economic challenges. But the European Union is also counting on the emergence of a strong figure in Berlin.

Of course, this is all connected to the election victory of Donald Trump. It will be necessary to stand up to the new American president, because his plans in the trade and security domains – both of which are crucial for Europe – are worrying. That being said, Trump will be wary of shooting himself in the foot. As a businessman, his thinking is more pragmatic than principled. Imposing massive tariffs on imports from Asia and Europe will lead to serious price rises in the US, which may result in an inflation spiral, whereas Trump was elected on a promise to control inflation. And while Trump's return to the White House is obviously not good news for Ukraine, he is not likely to drop NATO but will instead pressure it into spending more money on defence, which will benefit the American arms industry. These are considerations the president cannot ignore.

In other words, the great apocalypse is not (yet) just around the corner. It would therefore be unwise to lose ourselves in too much soul-searching and exaggerated masochism. After an unavoidable period of moaning and groaning about the election result, we need to focus on what we ourselves can do to defend our European interests as effectively as possible. With Trump, if we can. Against Trump, if we must.

To protect our exports to the US, we can probably best rely on Ursula von der Leyen. After all, she is the person responsible on behalf of the European Commission for external trade policy throughout the EU. For open economies like Belgium, Denmark, Ireland and the Netherlands it is crucial that the Commission takes the lead in these matters. In this way, it will not only be the interests of the larger member states that are taken into account. These larger countries have the advantage that they can negotiate directly with Trump and, as a result, perhaps get more favourable deals.

Who in Europe will restrain the growth of authoritarian tendencies now that Trump and his supporters have been given a substantial ego boost by the electorate? This is a task that the European Parliament and its president Roberta Metsola will have to take on. To a large extent this is something that the Parliament is already doing at the internal level by sidelining the radical right. The Parliament is also the ideal place for publicly highlighting the inconsistencies of national leaders like Viktor Orbán. Perhaps they should also invite the Dutch prime minister Dick Schoof. If he is called on to explain his plans to allow no further asylum applications in the Netherlands, it will soon become clear to all Europe that such a proposal is unenforceable and that outside of The Hague no one is interested in Trump-like solutions for European problems.

And who will tackle the thorny issue of defence? Probably 'the other Donald', as the former president of the European Council once described himself. The current prime minister of Poland is constantly active in the search for new alliances that will guarantee future financial and military support to Ukraine, now that there is a possibility that Trump will cut the flow of US weapons and aid. Moreover, Tusk is not only looking to France, the Baltic states and Northern Europe to find this support, but also wants to reestablish defence relations with the UK. Now that the moderate Keir Starmer is in Downing Street there is potentially room for negotiation, not in the least because the British prime minister is also interested in closer consultations with the EU on security matters.

And if things really get bad for the EU, Brussels can always send Georgia Meloni to Washington. The Italian prime minister is well known for being on good terms with Trump, but at the same time is also acceptable to her fellow colleagues in the European Council and to the traditional political families in Europe. Which is not the case, for example, with someone like Orbán.

It is also worth noting that von der Leyen, Tusk, Starmer and Meloni are all both pro-Ukraine and trans-Atlantic-minded. To this list can be added the new President of the European Council, Antonío Costa, the new High Representative of the Union for Foreign Affairs and Security Policy, Kaja Kallas, the NATO secretary-general, Mark Rutte, and the new German chancellor, Friedrich Merz. In short, a whole new generation of political leaders has recently emerged, who together are willing to defend Europe's interests and cannot simply be dismissed by Washington as 'anti-American'. And who knows? Perhaps this new Team Europe might be able to make things difficult for Donald Trump after all.

Conclusion

Our new responsibility

The Russian full-scale invasion of Ukraine has caused a facture whose damage is still visible. It is a historic turning point for the old, European continent. There is an era before and an era after 24 February 2022. It means that the EU can never return to the naivety of the past.

The war has made clear that the European model is under strong pressure.[57] From the outside in, by the refusal of the regime in Moscow to accept the choices made by its neighbouring countries in favour of Brussels and away from the unattractive, imperial and neo-colonial model of the Kremlin.[58] And from the inside out, by a hybrid struggle that is being conducted against western society by various means, including the dissemination of fake news, the launching of cyber attacks and election interference.[59]

At the same time, the European model is more popular than ever. None of the existing member states wishes to leave the EU and its waiting room is full of new candidates. They all prefer the 'European way of life'.[60] It is relatively easy to demonstrate that this model is superior. But precisely what this way of life entails is more difficult to define. Even so, with this publication I have attempted to examine and explain in a positive way the soul of the European integration process in its current phase.[61]

What the EU must do in the years ahead is not simply to undergo the results of the European integration process passively, but instead become the active defender of this process, both internally and externally. Internally, the Union will need to commit itself more than ever before to the concept of strategic autonomy, especially in the domains of energy, technology and defence.[62] To make its internal operation more effective and more efficient, the EU's institutions and decision-making procedures should ideally be overhauled at the same time. The member states must also make a greater effort to reach unified positions on key issues, starting with Germany and France.[63] Externally, a similar effort must be made to develop unified and assertive policies towards the most important geopolitical players in the world – the United States, Russia and China – and their respective allies. Our relations with other countries must also be deepened on the basis of conditionality. The days when Europe allowed itself to be blackmailed must be put behind us, once and for all. Of course, as a continent we will continue to be dependent in crucial areas (like natural resources) on other players, but we must not forget that we also have important trump cards in our hand – and we must not be afraid to play them. Respect for the EU in the wider world will have to be earned, but past diffidence about defending our interests, both internally and externally, must be replaced by a new self-confidence.

Within the context of the further future enlargement of the EU, these internal and external challenges will develop concurrently. The accession of new member states is probably the most underestimated form of active geopolitics.[64] The Union has the direction of this process in its own hands and is not limited by or dependent on other players. Moreover, the results of this enlargement policy will be highly successful and sustainable.[65] This means that the EU cannot and must not hide behind false arguments as a reason for doing nothing, but must instead accept and take responsibility for positive action. Future enlargement is the litmus test of the geopolitical role the EU wants to play. For once, Brussels is not depending on Washington, Moscow or Beijing. And is therefore able to decide on its own, showing the EU's courage to the whole continent.

Of course, we need to remember that in the decade following the shock of the financial crisis the performance of the EU was feeble. Following the accession of Croatia in 2013 – the longest period since accession since 1973, too little commitment was shown to other candidate countries in the Western Balkans. And since the Euromaidan protest in Kyiv – also in 2013 – the Union has also done little more than pay lip service to the Ukrainians. This weakness did not go unnoticed in Moscow.[66] The subsequent consequences have been severe: the annexation of Crimea, the war in Donbas, active support for Serbia and *Republika Srpska*, and the systematic destabilisation of the EU via the migrant crisis, Brexit and financial support for Russia-friendly parties. The pandemic brought a temporary halt to such measures, but they were resumed in 2022 with the full-scale invasion of Ukraine. This at least had the virtue (if no other) of at last opening the eyes of Western Europe to the true nature of Vladimir Putin's regime, not least for the Russian people: deceitful, criminal and violent. Kremlin lovers now know exactly who and what it is they are supporting. This is bad enough, but equally harmful are the criticism of the so-called moderate centre. How is it possible after almost three years of war that these useful idiots – because that is what they are to Putin – are still pleading for peace and reconciliation with Russia?

To protect the European way of life, the EU will have to toughen up its act. There is no shortage of plans, reports and declarations.[67] What seems to be lacking is the necessary decisiveness and political will. If the Union fails to take action in the near future, it will soon fall victim to the so-called 'expectations delivery gap' ('See? I told you the EU can't do it!'). This will give extra ammunition to the Union's critics and will further discourage its supporters. In addition to decisiveness, additional resources will also be necessary. Here again swift action is essential, otherwise another pitfall lies waiting: the 'expectations capabilities gap'.[68] If we do not give the EU the tools it needs to fulfil its new responsibilities, we will undermine not only the effectiveness but also the legitimacy of the integration process.[69]

Put simply, a radical new approach is necessary. After the fall of the Berlin Wall in 1989, the EU was able to develop into an instrument for expansion in a climate of relative calm. This was the era of political and economic globalisation. Since the Russian invasion of 2022, the new challenge is to develop the EU into an instrument of protection a hostile environment. This will require us to make difficult choices. The support that we give to the Ukrainian armed forces – which is actually the European army in action – must be continued undiminished and preferably increased.[70] It is also high time that Europe invests more in its own military security, in the full realisation that this will mean sacrificing some of our prosperity.[71] Likewise, we must accept that there are other domains, such as migration, where it will be the responsibility of the EU to clear up the mess that has been created. Salving our own conscience but looking away from the problems on the ground without offering workable solutions is a luxury that we can no longer afford.[72]

At first glance, this new approach seems diametrically opposed to the spirit of the times. We have forgotten how to make sacrifices, both individually and collectively.[73] But just as the loneliness and aimlessness in society cannot be tackled without breaking the taboo of hyper-individualisation, so it will not be possible to overcome political unease without first exposing a number of painful truths. In the demographic domain, for example, the EU faces a double problem: one the one hand, the need for massive labour immigration (from outside the Union) to maintain prosperity in Western Europe; on the other hand, the creeping depopulation of large parts of Central and Eastern Europe (something that the authoritarian rulers in these countries are not keen to be reminded of).[74] Reversing these trends and challenging existing conventions will take time and plenty of political courage.[75]

AM, SEEK, EDUCATE,
CHIEVE !

If successful, this will herald the end of a Europe that is 'sated, bloated and bored'. At the same time, we must avoid trying to return to the past, but without questioning our acquired social rights, such as equality, the protection of minorities and the rule of law. Nor should we listen to the politicians of many different persuasion who profess to uphold traditional and Christian values, while their words and deeds show that they have never read the Bible any further than the Old Testament.[76] Without succumbing to defeatism or to newfangled arrogance or to the nostalgic temptation to 'make Europe great again', Europe needs to reconnect with its character as a self-critical continent.[77] This is a task in which everyone – citizens and policy-makers alike – must take responsibility. We must all leave the safety of the castle and cross the drawbridge to rediscover the old city. But be in no doubt: stepping out of our comfort zone in this manner will not be easy and will generate resistance.[78]

Since Max Weber, we know that in public life (and therefore in politics) conviction often conflicts with responsibility. It is the task of academics (amongst others) to ensure that we do not lose sight of the side of conviction.[79] Or to put it in more secular, administrative terms: 'speaking truth to power'.[80] However, the reality is always more complex and unruly. 'When everything is in motion, it is important to keep a cool head.'[81] And to show understanding for the difficulties of political practice, but while keeping a firm grip on major principles.[82]

For their part, politicians must have the courage to speak the truth honestly and clearly. They must tell it like it is. Exaggerated pessimism will not help us and will only result in social demobilisation. Nor is leaving everything as it is a viable option. This kind of worrying complacency must be fought at all costs. In other words, it is clear that much needs to be done, but there is no reason to lose heart before we have even started.[83] Because we are much more resilient than we think.[84] For this reason, it is crucial at this turning point in European history that responsible politicians embody hope and belief that we can confront and overcome the challenges we face – and in this way reinvent ourselves as a brave old continent in this 21st century.

'You must want to imagine a better world. Can we do that? That is the key question. Is the pressure great enough for the imagining of a better world? (...) If death and destruction take hold, so that there no longer seems to be any light, this is often the moment when the most brilliant plans emerge – and also the strength to work them out practically.'[85]

A word of thanks

Telling, teaching and (a bit of) preaching. Since the publication of the first edition of *Why Europe?* I have been able to further refine my thoughts about the European integration process in numerous public readings, panel debates and (guest) lectures. I am grateful for the opportunities I have been given, amongst others by the KU Leuven and the Fund involvEU.

Every op-ed or column is a challenge to present a core message with convincing arguments to an interested reading public in a limited number of words. My thanks go to all the editorial teams who offered me this forum as a committed academic. I am especially grateful to the opinion editors of *De Tijd* (Franky Van Hamme and Anja Otte) and *De Standaard* (Hans Cottyn and Leni De Backer) and to the editors-in-chief at *Tertio* (Emmanuel Van Lierde and Johan Van der Vloet) for their smooth collaboration and useful feedback, as well as for their help in ensuring that these contributions to the debate about Europe at the crossroads can be read again here in this book.

A big thank you also goes to Bart Derwael for his generosity, encouragement, inspiration and patience. This applies equally to all his colleagues at Acco Publishing for their rapid transformation of my manuscript into print, including the translation from Dutch. I hope that the end result will appeal to many readers in Europe and beyond.

Last but not least, I owe a huge debt to Mathieu Segers, with whom I edited *The Cambridge History of the European Union* (CUP, 2 volumes, 2023). It was with him that I first shared and discussed my ideas about the superior model and meaning of 'the European way of life'. Sadly, he will never see the fruits of this intellectual exercise, but for me he will always be a much valued colleague, *compagnon de route* and friend. To him I dedicate this publication.

Photographs

Over the past few years I have had the opportunity to discover the European continent during various study trips: not only to the major EU capitals (Brussels, Luxembourg, Strasbourg and Frankfurt), but also to peripheral regions (like Northern Ireland and Cyprus) and to all the candidate countries. Everywhere I spoke with academics, politicians, diplomats and journalists, always taking detailed notes and lots of photographs. Some of these photos have been selected for this book.

p. 8: The EU flag on the wall opposite the entrance to Studio Europa Maastricht, where Mathieu Segers had his office (Onze Lieve Vrouweplein – Our Lady Square – in Maastricht, 13 May 2019).

p. 14: A 'You are EU' advertising poster at a bus stop in Mondello (Sicily, 31 December 2023).

p. 19: A statue of the Virgin Mary – *Virgo Europae Patrona* (Our Lady of Europe) – at the Notre-Dame-de-l'Europe chapel at Fleury-devant-Douaumont, the only building in an area of woodland, serving as a memorial to the village of that name which was totally destroyed during the Battle of Verdun in 1916 (20 July 2020).

p. 27: The Wall of Remembrance of the Fallen for Ukraine in Triokhsviatytelska Street: a monument to the soldiers who have died in the fight against Russia from 2014 onwards (Kyiv, 31 August 2022).

p. 42: A section of the Berlin Wall, gifted by the Germany Government to the people of Georgia and erected in its old capital city (Mtskheta, 16 September 2019).

p. 50: The flags of the EU member states and Ukraine at the entrance to the European Parliament (Strasbourg, 6 April 2022).

p. 60: A souvenir shop on Macedonia Square, between the house where Mother Theresa was born and a statue of Alexander the Great (Skopje, 9 March 2024).

p. 76: A 'World Help Us' banner on the sandbagged monument to Princess Olga in Mykhailivs'ka Square (Kyiv, 31 August 2022).

p. 86: The barrier at the entrance to Gazimestan, the tower commemorating the Battle of Kosovo, otherwise known as the Battle of the Field of Blackbirds (Pristina, 21 May 2023).

p. 100: The ICAR Canned Beef Monument (Sarajevo, 23 October 2023).

Notes

1   This publication is an updated translation of S. Van Hecke's *Het kantelende continent. Overleeft Europa de 21ste eeuw?* (A continent at the crossroads. Will Europe survive the 21st century?). Leuven: Acco, 2024, 142 p.

2   The text is a fully revised and expanded version of the sixth Johan Willem Beyen Lecture entitled 'Is the European model still superior?', which I gave on Friday 13 October 2023 at the University of Utrecht: https://www.uu.nl/agenda/is-the-european-model-still-superior-door-steven-van-hecke.

3   D.M. Herszenhorn & M. de la Baume, 'Outrage over "protecting our European Way of Life" job title', *Politico*, 11 September 2019: https://www.politico.eu/article/outrage-over-protecting-our-european-way-of-life-job-title/.

4   European Commission, 'Promoting our European way of life: Protecting our citizens and values', s.d.: https://commission.europa.eu/strategy-and-policy/priorities-2019-2024/promoting-our-european-way-life_en.

5   For references to Ukraine the Ukrainian spelling has been used, not the Russian.

6   '"Russia is trying to destroy the Ukrainian European way of life; we will not allow that" – President's speech at the special plenary session of the European Parliament', Brussels, 9 February 2023: https://www.president.gov.ua/en/news/ukrayinskij-yevropejskij-sposib-zhittya-rosiya-namagayetsya-80881.

7   I previously discussed the different narratives briefly in the predictive 'look ahead' article entitled 'Glazen Bol 2020-2030', *De Tijd*, 3 January 2020: https://www.tijd.be/opinie/algemeen/een-opwarmer-voor-europa/10195407.html.

8   Although the war only started in Northern and Western Europe in April (Denmark and Norway) and May (Belgium, France, Luxembourg and the Netherlands) 1940, it actually began on 1 September 1939 with the German invasion of Poland.

9   Along with peace and reconciliation, the EU's external security also suffered a serious blow, even though the Treaty of Maastricht (1993) had supposedly initiated a common foreign and security policy. A wave of terrorist attacks in 2015-2017 revealed that internal security was another of the Union's weak spots.

10 See https://www.nobelprize.org/prizes/peace/2012/ summary/. In its motivation the Nobel Prize Committee made no mention of the wars and armed conflicts that have taken place in Europe since 1945. In his *Imagining European unity since 1000 AD* (New York: Palgrave MacMillan, 2015) Patrick Pasture rightly pointed out that the colonial wars of the founding EU member states were also difficult to reconcile with the current peace story.

11 S. Van Hecke & W. Wolfs, 'Het democratisch surplus van de Europese Unie'. In: B. Pattyn, P. d'Hoine (eds.), *Identiteit in perspectief* (Lessen voor de XXIste eeuw, 25), Leuven: Leuven University Press, pp. 319-332.

12   He believed that economic and social cohesion formed the foundation of the
        'marriage contract' between the member states. See my In Memoriam article:
        S. Van Hecke, 'Een interne markt, een eenheidsmunt én een sociaal Europa:
        hoe Jacques Delors het verschil wist te maken', *De Morgen*, 29 December
        2023, p. 12: https://www.demorgen.be/meningen/een-interne-markt-een-
        eenheidsmunt-en-een-sociaal-europa-hoe-jacques-delors-het-verschil-wist-
        te-maken~bf68a8b4/.

13   See S. Van Hecke & K. Vermeylen, *Waarom Europa? Van vredesproject tot
        oorlog in Oekraïne*, Leuven: LannooCampus, 2022.

14   S. Van Hecke, 'Vrede door gerechtigheid. Enkele reflecties op de oorlog in
        Oekraïne'. In: *Collationes. Vlaams Tijdschrift voor Theologie en Pastoraal,*
        Vol. 53, No. 2, May 2023, pp. 199-213.

15   The war in Ukraine actually started in 2014 with the Russian invasion of
        Donetsk and Loehansk, followed by the annexation of Crimea. Even so, for
        the turning point I refer consistently to 2022.

16   At least as far as the politicians of regimes in the Global South are concerned.
        In practice, Europe continues to be an ideal for many Africans, Asians and
        Latin Americans. The EU is the destination they want to reach in their search
        for a safer and better future.

17   Together with *Republika Srpska*, the Serbian entity in Bosnia and
        Herzegovina, where Milorad Dodik holds power, thanks to the support of
        Vučić.

18   The other three countries in the Western Balkans are Bosnia and
        Herzegovina, Kosovo and Serbia.

19   Critics argue that, amongst other things, the EU Neighbourhood Policy and
        other Brussels-supported initiatives like the European Political Community
        have been launched specifically to keep countries sweet with alternatives to
        full membership.

20   This is the so-called 'merit-based approach'. Officially, progress in the field of
        integration is judged on the basis of merit. In other words, whoever meets the
        conditions is automatically rewarded. In practice, however, it always comes
        down to a political decision.

21   After a train journey from the border town of Przemyśl lasting several hours,
        I finally arrived in the Ukrainian capital after dark. Because of the curfew, no
        one could leave the central station. With no SIM card, no cash money and no
        knowledge of the Ukrainian language, I was worried that I might find myself
        in trouble. Fortunately, I was able to pay for the toilet with my credit card.
        See S. Van Hecke, 'Bezoek aan Kyiv, Irpin en Bucha: een reisverslag', *KU
        Leuven Blogt*, 2 September 2022: https://kuleuvenblogt.be/2022/09/02/
        bezoek-aan-kyiv-irpin-en-bucha-een-reisverslag/.

22   See, for example: 'When we build Europe, we will build freedom' – online
        speech by President Volodymyr Zelenskyy at the Ukraine Recovery
        Conference in London, 21 June 2023: https://www.president.gov.ua/
        en/news/koli-mi-zbuduyemo-ukrayinu-mi-zbuduyemo-svobodu-onlajn-
        vistu-83705.

23   Article 50 of the Treaty on European Union. For ease of reference, we will use
        the name by which this treaty is most commonly known: the Treaty of Lisbon.

24   In 2004 and 2007 twelve new member states joined the Union, while the
        Treaty of Lisbon only came into force in 2009.

25   Nor is it anything to do with European civilisation. In my opinion, this is
      a controversial term, which is more inclined to lead to misunderstanding
      than to produce clarity. Nevertheless, see the interview with the French
      politician Clément Beaune, in which he says: 'I believe the great European
      battle is cultural and civilizational, not against anyone, but for certain
      values'. R. Cohen, 'Europe's "tormented history" drives an ambitious Macron
      protégé', *The New York Times*, 1 September 2023: https://www.nytimes.
      com/2023/09/01/world/europe/france-politics-clement-beaune.html.
26   Article 2 of the Treaty on European Union. See: https://eur-lex.europa.eu/
      legal-content/NL/TXT/HTML/?uri=CELEX:12012M002.
27   Hence the *Universal* Declaration of Human Rights and the (European)
      Convention for the Protection of Human Rights and *Fundamental* Freedoms
      (ECHR). Whoever defends anything else ultimate ends up in relativism.
28   But of course you do need the EU for enforceability, via the ECHR for the
      member states of the Council of Europe and the Charter of Fundamental
      Rights of the European Union for the EU member states.
29   For this reason, constitutional patriotism – the idea that people form
      a political community because they all profess the norms and values
      of a pluralistic, liberal democracy (as an alternative to nationalism or
      cosmopolitanism), as is the case in the EU –whose leading advocate is the
      German philosopher Jürgen Habermas, is also unable to offer the necessary
      solace.
30   Article 3 of the Treaty on European Union. See: https://eur-lex.europa.eu/
      legal-content/NL/TXT/HTML/?uri=CELEX%3A12008M003.
31   Q. Peel, 'Merkel warns on cost of welfare', *Financial Times*, 16 December
      2012: https://www.ft.com/content/8ccof584-45fa-11e2-b7ba-00144feabdc0.
      Note that Merkel refers to 'way of life'. And also that social spending is not
      'European' policy, because this is a competence of the individual members
      states, and not the EU.
32   Of course, this is simply a matter of elementary arithmetic. Together,
      Germany and France are good for more than 40% of the EU's GNP.
      Adding the Benelux countries takes this figure to over 50%. See: https://
      www.statista.com/statistics/1373419/eu-gdp-percentage-share-member-
      state-2022/.
33   See the Draghi Report on 'The future of European competitiveness'
      (September 2024).
34   As in so many policy domains, much depends on the implementation and the
      enforceability.
35   An interesting contribution to the history of the European integration
      project and in particular its trans-Atlantic roots was provided in Mathieu
      Segers' most recent English-language monograph: M. Segers, *The Origins of
      European Integration. The Pre-History of Today's European Union, 1937-
      1951*, Cambridge: CUP, 2023, 255p.
36   Article 17 of the Treaty on the Functioning of the European Union: https://
      www.europarl.europa.eu/at-your-service/nl/be-heard/religious-and-non-
      confessional-dialogue.
37   See: https://www.leuenberg.eu/.

38 See: https://www.comece.eu/eu-bishops-empower-young-people-and-launch-the-comece-youth-net/.

39 P. Steinz, *Made in Europe. De kunst die ons continent bindt*, Amsterdam: Uitgeverij Nieuw Amsterdam, 2014.

40 See: https://nieuwamsterdam.nl/producten/made-europe-9789046819258.

41 See: https://studioeuropamaastricht.nl/nl/project/ the-european-review-of-books/.

42 G. Riotta, Interview with Umberto Eco: 'It's culture, not war, that cements European identity'. *The Guardian*, 26 January 2012: https://www.theguardian.com/world/2012/jan/26/umberto-eco-culture-war-europa.

43 O. Boehme, *Scepsis. Over wankelend vooruitgangsgeloof*, Brussels: ASP, 2023, p. 96: 'The explicit cultivation of all distinctions between origins, religions, skin colours and convictions has led to a situation in which only one consensus remains: namely, that everyone has his or her own truth'. [translation from Dutch]

44 T.G. Ash, *Europa. Een persoonlijke geschiedenis*, Amsterdam: Geus, 2023, p. 259.

45 See the chapter 'Waarom bestaat er geen Europees leger?' in S. Van Hecke & K. Vermeylen, *Waarom Europa? Van vredesproject tot oorlog in Oekraïne*, Leuven: LannooCampus, 2022, pp. 19-42.

46 Note that Zelenskyy made the same choice when faced with a similar dilemma. Rather than burying the hatchet with Russia, renouncing EU and NATO membership and giving in to the demands of Moscow, he opted resolutely for a free and Western-oriented Ukraine. With all the consequences we now know for his own country and for the rest of Europe.

47 And also that NATO should continue to exist. When it was founded 40 years earlier, in 1949, its purpose (according to its first secretary-general, Lord Hastings Lionel Ismay) was 'to keep the Americans in, the Russians out and the Germans down'. https://www.nato.int/cps/en/natohq/declassified_137930.htm.

48 This resonates with the famous saying of Thomas Mann: 'We do not want a German Europe, but a European Germany.'

49 Since then, the peripheral countries have been listened to more attentively and are no longer regarded as second rank.

50 At the informal EU summit about defence, taking place on 3 February 2025 in Brussels, the NATO secretary-general was the main guest.

51 For more on the fight against FIMI (Foreign Information Manipulation and Interference), see my op-ed 'Europese verkiezingen dreigen toch spannend te worden', *De Tijd*, 16 February 2024: https://www.tijd.be/opinie/algemeen/europese-verkiezingen-dreigen-toch-spannend-te-worden/10526952.html.

52 S. Van Hecke, 'Less Europe in a larger union: Belgium and its old and new eastern neighbours'. In: M. Gehler & M. Graf (eds.), *Europa und die deutsche Einheit: Beobachtungen, Entscheidungen und Folgen*, Göttingen: Vandenhoeck & Ruprecht, 2017, pp. 505-520.

53 Of course, the extent to which this priority was correctly implemented and achieved sufficient results in practice is open to discussion.

54 S. Van Hecke, 'Welke samenleving willen wij zijn?', *De Tijd*, 19 March 2022, p. 23: https://www.tijd.be/opinie/analyse/welke-samenleving-willen-we-zijn/10374685.html.

55   Note that this criticism of the West shows parallels with radical Islamism.

56   S. Van Hecke, 'Hoelang nog kan Europa zijn achtertuin negeren?', *De Standaard*, 15 September 2017, p. 37.

57   R. Verrycken, interview with political commentator Ivan Krastvev: 'There is no new Cold War'. *De Tijd*, 16 September 2023, p. 19. 'This war is also a European war, as well as a nationalist one. It makes us realise that we are nowhere without European unity'. [translation from Dutch

58   K. Welle, 'Le nouveau visage des droites en Europe et le conservatisme du futur', *Le Grand Continent*, 30 May 2023, https://legrandcontinent. eu/fr/2023/05/30/le-nouveau-visage-des-droites-en-europe-et-le-conservatisme-du-futur/: 'Today, the European continent is structured by two main principles: in the east there is the expression of Russia's colonial and imperial ambitions; in the west and the centre there is a union of citizens and states that offers shelter and protection, as well as relations founded on the rule of law.' [translation from French]

59   S. Van Hecke, 'Europese verkiezingen dreigen toch spannend te worden', *De Tijd*, 17 February 2024, p. 23.

60   'Europeans who are not yet members of the EU can describe and explain the European dream perfectly. It is a dream of prosperity, peace and security, which they hope can be achieved as soon as possible. But for the Europeans who have been members for a long time the EU has become either an abstract reality of which they are hardly aware or a bureaucratic monster that interferes too much in their lives. I find this fascinating.' These are the words of writer Robert Menasse, whose book *Die Erweiterung* won the the 17th European Book Prize at the end of 2023. D. Illegems, 'De Europese nachtmerrie van Romancier Robert Menasse', *Humo*, 19 March 2024, p. 134. [translation from Dutch]

61   For a 'negative' definition – the European integration process as collective insurance against the vulnerability of the European continent – see: S. Van Hecke & K. Vermeylen, *Waarom Europa? Van vredesproject tot oorlog in Oekraïne*, Leuven: LannooCampus, 2022, p. 200: 'The integration process protects Europe against its vulnerability at the global level. At the same time, the EU protects its member states – and in particular the smaller ones – against their vulnerability within Europe.' [translation from Dutch]

62   How this transformed the EU is convincingly described in: M. De Vos, *Grootmacht Europa. De omwenteling van de Europese Unie*, Antwerp: Ertsberg, 2023, p. 71: '(...) the European Union was a bastion of the free market, but is now becoming a bastion of statification and politicisation.' [translation from Dutch]

63   S. Van Hecke, 'Frans-Duitse as is aan fundamentele reset toe', *De Tijd*, 15 March 2024, p. 23.

64   M. De Vos, *Grootmacht Europa. De omwenteling van de Europese Unie*, Antwerp: Ertsberg, 2023, p. 28: 'The enlargement of the European Union must not be a purely passive process that spontaneously draws eager and suitable candidates into the European fold. It must be a strategic process that presses hesitant countries firmly and proactively to the European bosom on the basis of a conscious European strategic-geographic positioning.' [translation from Dutch]

65   Look at the example of the Baltic states, the darlings of the European
      integration process. Until 1991, they were part of the Soviet Union. Today,
      Estonia, Latvia and Lithuania have become exemplary EU member states
      in many different areas. For example, they joined the euro zone during the
      financial crisis and they score consistently high for digitalisation. Their
      success undermines the argument, often put forward by Viktor Orbán, that
      countries from Central and Eastern Europe are 'different' from the rest of
      the continent because of their communist past and therefore have a right to
      'special' treatment.

66   There is an interesting link here with the Middle East. Putin correctly
      understood the 'disengagement' signal sent out by the West and by the US
      in particular, seeing this as a blank cheque that allowed him to play a highly
      controversial and ruthless role in the Syrian civil war. The unwillingness
      of the West to intervene militarily, even when there was clear evidence of
      breaches of international and military law, possibly encouraged Putin to
      believe that 'the decadent West' would not respond adequately to a full-
      scale invasion of Ukraine. He interpreted the West's non-intervention for
      humanitarian reasons as a sign of weakness.

67   The 'Budapest Declaration on the New European Competitiveness Deal' (8
      November 2024) serves as the latest example.

68   In EU jargon this is known as 'capacity to act'. It sounds even better in
      German: *Handlungsfähigkeit*.

69   In this respect, the EU's moment of truth is approaching rapidly: the debate
      about 'own resources' and the Multiannual Financial Framework 2028-2034.
      This will not only involve heated discussions about more financial resources
      but also about a shift from the member states to the EU and within policy
      domains on the basis of new priorities. S. Van Hecke, 'Quo vadis Europa?
      Follow the Money!', *De Tijd*, 17 June 2023, p. 23.

70   T. Huhtanen, 'The war in Ukraine, 2 years on. In 2024, Europe must decide
      if it wants to win,' 24 February 2024. (https://www.linkedin.com/pulse/
      war-ukraine-2-years-2024-europe-must-decide-wants-win-tomi-huhtanen-
      mkl1e/): 'Currently, Ukraine's army IS the European army, serving as a
      frontline defence for Europe's security, its values, and its future. (...) In war,
      like politics, persistence and determination are key elements.'

71   That a pacifist Social Democrat is now suddenly arguing in favour of a
      European army is a striking example of this turnaround: K. Van Brempt,
      De comeback van Europa: Na de crisissen, de toekomst, 2023, Antwerp:
      Erstberg, p. 138.

72   S. Van Hecke, 'Dirty deals', *Tertio*, 23 August 2023, p. 5.

73   P. De Keyzer, 'Weg met "nu, nu, nu"', *De Tijd*, 18 August 2022: https://www.
      tijd.be/dossiers/de-prullenmand/weg-met-nu-nu-nu/10408177.html.

74   S. Van Hecke, 'Wat rijmt op democratie en economie?', *De Tijd*, 27 November
      2023, p. 23.

75   S. Van Hecke, '"Het keren van de tanker', België omarmt Europa', *Knack
      Special*, 21 December 2023, p. 66.

76   In other words, regimes like Viktor Orbán's are a permanent insult for every
      self-respecting nationalist, conservative and right-leaning Christian. S. Van
      Hecke, 't Is de hypocrisie, stupid!', *De Tijd*, 25 June 2021, p. 11.

77   'Europe is the only continent that engages in genuine self-criticism',
     [translation from Dutch], according to writer Robert Menasse in F.
     Huysegems, 'De teloorgang van de wereldgeest. Interview: Robert Menasse,
     of Oostenrijk zonder eigenschappen', *De Standaard*, 25 April 2002: https://
     www.standaard.be/cnt/dexa25042002_017.

78   O. Boehme, *Scepcis. Over wankelend vooruitgangsgeloof,* Brussels: ASP,
     2023, p. 153: 'Consequently, this uncertainty and sombreness puts wind
     in the sails of diverse movements: climate activism, wokers, extreme right,
     extreme left, and fanatical nationalism.' [translation from Dutch]

79   In his memoires Wilfried Martens quoted extensively from *Politics and Belief*
     by the Protestant French philosopher Paul Ricoeur: 'Here we are concerned
     with a remarkably fruitful distinction that I borrow from the great German
     sociologist from the beginning of the century, Max Weber. In his famous
     essay *Politik als Beruf* he distinguishes two levels of ethical behaviour: "the
     ethics of conviction" –*Gesinnungsethik, morale de la conviction* – as he
     calls it and "the ethics of responsibility" – *Verantwortungsethik, morale
     de la responsabilité.* It is not without importance to know that in his first
     manuscript version Weber wrote "the ethics of power". This clarification
     is of very considerable significance for what follows, because it is my belief
     that the well-being of a community is ultimately based on the correctness
     of the relationship between these two ethics. On the one hand, there is the
     ethics of conviction, which is vested in scientific, academic and cultural
     associations, including the church, which make their own contributions in
     this domain – and not in the domain where politics is made. (...) On the other
     hand, there is the ethics of responsibility, which is also the ethics of the use
     of power, regulated violence and calculated guilt. It is my opinion that the
     task of political formations is to maintain a tension between these two moral
     forces. Because if we allow the ethics of conviction to coincide with the ethics
     of responsibility we will lapse into *Realpolitik*, into a Machiavellianism,
     which stems from the constant confusion of means and ends. If, on the other
     hand, the ethics of conviction would arrogate to itself some kind of direct
     interference, then we would lapse into all the illusions of moralism and
     clericalism.' See: Wilfried Martens, *De memoires. Luctor et emergo*, Tielt:
     Lannoo, p. 89. [translation from Dutch]

80   See, for example: M. Brans, 'Speaking truth to power?', *Res Publica*, Vol. 58,
     No. 3, 2016, pp. 363-369.

81   A. De Greef, 'Laten we het hoofd koel houden', *De Standaard*, 16 March
     2024, p. 56.

82   According to Albert Camus: 'One must place one's principles in big things.
     For the small, mercy will suffice.' When it really comes down to it, I find the
     grey zone 'comfortable but complacent, and not very courageous'. See: L.
     Verpoest, 'Sabelslijpers en vredesstichters', *De Standaard*, 22 March 2024, p.
     36.

83   In the words of Hans-Gert Pöttering, former president of the European
     Parliament and the *Konrad-Adenauer-Stiftung*: 'We are better than we think
     but not good enough.'

84   J. Leenders, 'Dreigt er echt oorlog? De waarschuwingen klinken luid en
     duidelijk: "We moeten ons meer en beter voorbereiden"', *De Limburger*, 31
     December 2023, pp. 2-3.

85   According to the professor of European history at the University of
       Maastricht, Mathieu Segers, in his final interview: P. Giesen, 'Voor moreel
       leiderschap moet je je een betere wereld willen voorstellen. Kan Europa
       dat?', *De Volkskrant*, 1 December 2023: https://www.volkskrant.nl/nieuws-
       achtergrond/voor-moreel-leiderschap-moet-je-je-een-betere-wereld-willen-
       voorstellen-kan-europa-dat~b93a182a/. [translation from Dutch]

www.ingramcontent.com/pod-product-compliance
Ingram Content Group UK Ltd.
Pitfield, Milton Keynes, MK11 3LW, UK
UKHW021818150726
7214IPUK00017B/184

9 789464 678062